THE ADAMS
COLLEGE
ADMISSIONS
ESSAY
HANDBOOK

Tips and Techniques to
Give Your Application the Edge

Burton Jay Nadler and Jordan Nadler

▲

Adams Media
Avon, Massachusetts

Published by
Adams Media, an F+W Publications Company
57 Littlefield Street, Avon, MA 02322. U.S.A.
www.adamsmedia.com

ISBN: 1-59337-058-X

Printed in Canada.

J I H G F E D C B A

Library of Congress Cataloging-in-Publication Data
Nadler, Burton Jay
The Adams college admissions essay handbook /
Burton Jay Nadler and Jordan Nadler.
p.   cm.
ISBN 1-59337-058-X
1. College applications--United States--Handbooks, manuals, etc.
2. Universities and colleges--United States--Admission--Handbooks,
manuals, etc. 3. Exposition (Rhetoric)--Handbooks, manuals, etc.
I. Title: College admissions essay handbook. II. Nadler, Jordan. III. Title.
LB2351.52.U6N33   2004
378.1'616--dc22   2003028020

This publication is designed to provide accurate and authoritative information with regard to the subject matter covered. It is sold with the understanding that the publisher is not engaged in rendering legal, accounting, or other professional advice. If legal advice or other expert assistance is required, the services of a competent professional person should be sought.
—From a *Declaration of Principles* jointly adopted by a Committee of the American Bar Association and a Committee of Publishers and Associations

Many of the designations used by manufacturers and sellers to distinguish their products are claimed as trademarks. Where those designations appear in this book and Adams Media was aware of a trademark claim, the designations have been printed in initial capital letters.

This book is available at quantity discounts for bulk purchases.
For information, call 1-800-872-5627.

Dedication

To grandmothers, great-uncles, and great-aunts, who often are the ones who make college admissions dreams realities.

To Justin and Rachel, the next members of our family to write essays and, ultimately, transform admissions dreams into their own personal and educational realities.

To Gwen and Bill of the University of Rochester, who help transform the dreams of many into eclectic realities. The colors of this school are blue and yellow. Appropriately, these hues blend to make "green," the name shared by these two individuals who personify this amazing institution and its motto of "meliora"— always better!

To high school friends Betsy, Abby, Jud, Shelli, and Bruce, who supported the essay writing and emotional needs related to college admissions, and who will always be remembered for dreams dreamt and realities forever positively shared.

To those whose essays appear as samples in this publication. Your willingness to share will inspire others to transform essay dreams into well-crafted drafts and finished realities. Our thanks to James Dollinger-McElligott, Kelly DuBois, Philip Driggs Fileri, Svenja Gudell, Claudia Guinot, Peter Kunhardt, Ugochi Okorie, Enyinne Ijeoma Owunwanne, Elena Rabinovitch, Zera Fatima Rizavi, Carl Philip Emmanuel Rosenthal, Jyotsna Singh, Guan-Lu Zhang.

Contents

Introduction
Who, What, When, and Why
You Should Read This Book

IF YOU ARE READING *The Adams College Admissions Essay Handbook*, you are not alone! Literally millions of high school students like you are investing time and all of their energy in college applications and admissions essays. Just like you, they seek to maximize the chances of being accepted into the school of their choice.

Anxiety, frustration, and negative thinking often accompany admissions efforts, particularly the essay writing part. But if you follow the tips and techniques offered in this handbook, you will surely cure your admissions and essay writing blues. *The Adams College Admissions Essay Handbook* will be your quick and easy Rx for success!

Maybe you are a high school junior, getting started early, and inspired by internal forces or not so subtle external motivators (Mom and Dad). Or, you are a senior, with deadlines pending and, perhaps, palpitations starting. Does the phrase "college admissions essay" send chills up and down your spine? When asked "Have you started yet?" do you quickly change the subject or mumble the obligatory "soon" and glare so the questioner realizes he or she should not have asked? As you continue to read, you will prepare to take important next steps on your path to success. The pages that follow will diminish anxieties and facilitate actions. Please read, follow the approaches presented, and then "do the write thing."

If you are an English teacher or college counselor, you can incorporate content and techniques presented here into one-on-one, group counseling, or classroom efforts. *The Adams College Admissions Essay Handbook* can be used as a text for courses and seminars, or to guide those who you individually tutor. It is designed to transform the concerns and confusion of students and parents into a very positive experience for all.

If you are a parent purchasing this book for your college-bound student, forget you ever saw it once you give it to your son or daughter. Parents always have the best interests of their children in mind, yet sometimes your kids misinterpret your efforts. Love, support, and inspire your essayist, but please do not pressure or try to serve as an editor. Remain a source of praise and positive reinforcement, as well as a sympathetic ear and friendly voice, but don't attempt to take on the role of essay writing counselor or critic. The authors and contributors of this book can, through literary voice, safely serve in these capacities. Following this advice will save you from major headaches and probably more than one unhappy scene.

What Makes This Book So Valuable?

No matter who the reader is, this book is intended to eliminate procrastination, diminish perspiration, enhance motivation, maximize inspiration, and prompt action! As you read, you will be encouraged to act immediately and to enjoy the self-expression that comes with essay writing. As you progress step by step, your anxieties will be reduced and your misconceptions regarding this process will be eliminated. You will find each subsequent action easier as you become motivated and put forth greater effort in writing the best essay that you can. Don't view admissions essay writing as an academic or lengthy process, but rather as your way to share views with readers and express thoughts and attitudes that will yield admissions success.

When Should You Begin Writing Your Essay?

This book will simplify essay writing, inspire actions, and guide you through the essay writing process using step-by-step approaches. If you are truly going to succeed at writing your college admissions essay, you must do it in a timely manner. By reading this introduction, you've taken the first step. Follow the tips and techniques presented here. Start now!

No matter where you apply, you must present your writing skills by crafting the best possible piece of writing to support your application. Your writing should surpass the competence shown in your SAT score or GPA. Your essay will invite others to judge your qualifications. It will prove that you're not just a piece of paper or another faceless candidate. Don't put off the process, no matter how early it may seem, how scared you feel, how difficult you might think it will be, or how uninspired you might be. While you might think, and often say, "I work best under pressure," the truth is that you don't. Leaving essays to the last minute will not allow you to maximize your efforts. You will not have the time to personalize essays for individual schools or obtain potentially useful advice from peers and teachers. By following the advice in this book, you will become aware of the necessary tasks that will, ultimately, yield the best efforts possible. Don't wait!

The Adams College Admissions Essay Handbook contains the perspectives of my daughter, Jordan, currently a junior at Cornell. Because she recently completed the college admissions process, we thought it would be very appropriate, important, and inspirational if she coauthored this work. This handbook also shares the wisdom of an English teacher/college counselor who coaches and edits students' essays. Advice from admissions professionals who have read and rated countless college admissions essays rounds out the book.

I have been a career services professional for a quarter century. Within career services roles at the University of Rochester, University of the Pacific, Dartmouth College, and Southern Methodist University, I learned to listen to students and translate their concerns and goals into action steps to help them reach their desired outcomes. I have written numerous books and articles on job search–related topics, including goal setting, resume writing, internship searching, and interviewing. For more than two decades, I have interacted with prospective higher education students, parents, admissions professionals, and college counselors. Inspired by many admissions-related responsibilities, by Jordan's past activities, and by the fact that my son, Justin, will go through the admissions process in the future, I applied all that I have learned about helping students to the specific objectives of this book.

Other contributors include Robert Massa, vice president for Enrollment, Student Life and College Relations at Dickinson College; and Bridget Klenk, assistant director of college counseling and English teacher at Flint School in Oakton, Virginia. Robert's background in admissions and financial aid spans time, geography, and multiple responsibilities. He has held various impressive titles at equally impressive schools, including Johns Hopkins, Colgate, and Union College. Colleagues within higher education have benefited from his mentorship and expertise for decades. Now, he will share strategies for success with you.

Bridget recently transitioned from the role of admissions professional to counselor and teacher. For years, she, traveled throughout the country educating applicants and, when that time of the year arrived, reading and rating hundreds of applications and essays. As a college counselor, Bridget offers you advice regarding when and how to plan and implement your overall admissions strategy and how to create the best essay in a timely manner. As a teacher, Bridget will inspire your essay writing creativity and focus on style, structure, and content. As an admissions officer, she will also share secrets about which essays kept her reading into the wee hours of the morning, and which ones made her fall asleep.

Robert and I will both offer perspectives of parents. His daughter, Haley, is currently a sophomore at the University of Rochester. Parents can be positive influences on overall admissions and, specifically, on essay writing and decision-making. Bridget will share sensitivities gained by interacting with parents as well.

Jordan will always remind you that this book is yours, not ours. *The Adams College Admissions Essay Handbook* is written to facilitate your actions and positive outcomes.

We all agree that positive input of educators, advocates, friends, and family can diminish angst and inspire action! Our carefully and strategically selected words will take you step by step toward success.

More often than not, information shared by all contributors will be presented in the voice of the author. To avoid confusion, whenever a contributor's or coauthor's actual comments are presented, they will be preceded by a name noted in bold lettering. An example:

Jordan states:

A book like this would be used as a reference guide, but only if it is easy to use and quick to finish. During senior year there are so many, many, many things to do and lots of stress caused by college applications. And junior year isn't much less hectic. Time is always a factor. I would have used a book like this if I knew I could turn to it for helpful, yet concise pointers presented in a relaxed way. I needed helpful "How do I get started?" and "How do I get finished?" hints—something to get me going. I didn't need more stress.

This book will share with you how to successfully transform essays you have already written for other purposes into college admissions essays. The best essays I wrote were ones I didn't know would end up being part of my college applications. There was less pressure and I was more inspired by self-expression and the purpose of the assignment. Admissions essay writers don't have to start from scratch!—*JN*

This approach will become familiar fairly quickly. Overall, the expertise and concerns shared by all of us will be very clear as you read. Ultimately, the varied opinions will blend to reveal common tips and techniques needed for you to succeed. You will be admitted to great schools, and you will decide which one is best for you to attend. You will continue on your already well-established path to success. Read, write, and succeed!

1 | Admissions:
It's Not Rocket Science Even If You Are Applying to MIT

"IT WAS THE BEST OF TIMES. It was the worst of times." Didn't one of those classic novels I read in high school start with those words? For too many, these two sentences accurately describe college admissions. With proper planning, a positive attitude, and strategic actions, you can avoid negative experiences associated with college admissions. Someday soon you will look back upon all that was involved with selecting, visiting, and applying to colleges and universities with fond memories. Anticipating the worst? You can ensure the best!

Proper planning begins during the junior year of high school. It involves evaluating your overall academic status as well as cocurricular profile, identifying target schools, initiating introspection, and even taking an "acronym-labeled aptitude test," including the PSAT. As you progress through your junior year to the fall of your senior year, planning involves additional self-assessment; scheduling time for numerous campus visits; and communicating directly with counselors, parents, alumni, teachers, coaches, and peers. Each action and interaction will contribute to active evaluation of your potential for admissions to specific institutions and narrowing down your list of schools. Later on during your junior or early in your senior year, you take "those tests," SAT or ACT, as well as SAT II and AP exams, and undertake more focused planning. This planning is proactive, not passive, involving data collection, analysis, brainstorming, and information exchanges with family, friends, faculty, counselors, coaches, admissions professionals, and students attending specific schools.

A positive attitude enhances the potential for a desired outcome. Pressures to find the perfect school or enroll in the highest-ranked institution are sources of consternation and procrastination rather than motivation. The self-assessment, exploratory, and self-expression components of admissions should prove very rewarding when seen in the proper perspective. You are in control of all exploration, evaluation, and communication efforts that will yield success. You, not others, will apply and be admitted to the schools of your choice. You will, with the help of others and resources like this book, complete all steps with ease and diminished concerns.

Strategic actions will be simplified to mini-steps. These begin with formal self-assessment and institutional profiling and end with submission of all required materials, including recommendations, transcripts, and test scores. At first, you'll expand small lists of potential schools and, later, will hone down lengthy lists. You'll make visits; complete and submit application documentation, including essays; and then you will receive offers of admissions. You will identify deadlines, follow to-do checklists, consult counselors, and address details. Simply put, during the months and weeks involved you will finish applications online or via printed forms, submit them to schools, and you will be admitted. Ultimately, you will make a decision to attend a great school and you will be a successful college student. It's truly that simple!

Essay writing is an important component of the overall process of admissions. Those who have already written many essays and papers will apply existing skills to targeted tasks ahead.

Admissions essays are not too different from those you have written for English, history, or government classes. Tips and techniques associated with creating the best admissions essays are easy to follow. Overall, the admissions exploration and application process is easier than many believe. Truly, the admissions process is not rocket science. Everyone can apply to and receive offers to enroll in the best schools. Soon, you will develop, fine-tune, and implement the best admissions strategy. By the time you finish this book you will be prepared to write the very best essays.

As you progress, you will become familiar with the importance of the traditional five-paragraph, 500-word essay and with other styles, strategies, and techniques. You will learn easy-to-follow steps to essay writing and admissions success. Many of your essays will be about the same length, and often will follow a format similar to the paragraphs that begin this chapter.

Don't put off any steps associated with admissions or essay writing. It is natural to avoid the unknown, but knowledge of all steps associated with admissions and essay writing will allow you to properly plan and implement each. No matter when or where you apply, you will soon develop and submit the best pieces of writing to support all applications. By following the advice in this book, you will become aware of all related tasks and soon yield the very, very best results. Don't wait. This is the best time to start.

The worst excuses I've heard to delay admissions activities include:

- It's too early.
- It's too late.
- It's too hard.
- I'm too busy.
- I don't have anyone to help me.
- I don't have a car and my parents can't take me on visits.
- I've never heard of these places.

- I'll never get in where I want to attend.
- Schools don't have applications ready yet.
- No one from my school ever goes to a good college.

It's never too early, even if materials are not ready to be distributed to applicants. You can conduct in-person or cyber visits to begin the fact gathering needed to ensure success at any time. You can begin inventorying "first impressions and intuitions" at any time. In this Web and e-mail age, you can gather information and communicate with anyone, including faculty, admissions professionals, and students currently attending each school. Resources like this book are easily accessible and, most important, parents, teachers, and peers are always ready to offer advice and support. Don't be afraid to ask for help, at any time.

If lack of information diminishes your motivation for immediate action, increased knowledge will truly be inspirational. Accurate and honest information will instill realistic attitudes. Admissions actions truly do not require very much time or energy. In fact, actions associated with applying to one school are repeated for others, and it is as easy to apply to two as it is to apply to twenty-two. Each candidate should confidently present unique qualifications, optimistic that schools re-evaluate their admissions criteria each year and evaluate one candidate at a time.

Maximize your chances by utilizing all of the information and advice contained in this handbook. Common misconceptions and negative beliefs, including those presented as excuses, cause unneeded anxiety and inspire procrastination rather than actions. These overgeneralizations, exaggerations, and clearly false expressions create delayed action and time wasting. Make a promise to yourself that you will focus on positive or clearly realistic expectations, not negative self-statements. The following affirmations should inspire your successful planning, positive attitudes, and strategic actions:

- I will quickly create, then expand, and later fine-tune a list of schools I would like to explore.
- I will immediately begin initial Web explorations of schools on my target list.
- I will soon share my activities with, and seek the advice of, a college counselor.
- I will soon visit the nearest private and public colleges or universities, explore options offered by each, and seek the guidance of an admissions counselor, as a base-line first step.
- I will identify a formal counselor or informal advisor with whom I will regularly communicate.
- I will make and follow a list of deadlines and things to do for each school I apply to.
- I will draft and finalize essays, using advice and strategies contained in this handbook.
- I will maintain a positive attitude when exploring schools, visiting campuses, and communicating with parents, teachers, counselors, and friends regarding admissions activities.
- I will finish and submit all applications at least thirty days prior to each deadline.
- I will focus on learning style, curriculum, and course offerings when determining which offer to accept.

For strategic planning and motivational purposes it is best to view the overall admissions process as a series of easy-to-complete steps. You may not be too surprised to learn that many of them parallel the affirmations that we just listed. The steps include:

- Assessment of personal educational interests, learning style, geographic preferences, and school-specific knowledge.
- Developing an initial list of schools to explore, matching self-assessment findings, and including recommendations of family, friends, counselors, and teachers.

- Undertaking Web explorations of schools, including much more than admissions links—to expand initial listings and prepare for visits. Use megasites like *www.petersons.com* for initial exploration and specific academic or student service department links of each school for more detailed research. Also click and explore career centers, academic advising, and overseas studies links as well.

- Visiting convenient private and public colleges and universities to build momentum and fine-tune exploration skills and techniques; then visiting as many schools as possible.

- Communicating regularly with parents, siblings, and peers to generate ideas; visiting school or private college counselors, teachers, or admissions professionals for formal advice and strategic support.

- Creating a final target list of schools, clearly noting deadlines and things to do for each.

- Completing all documentation, then submitting all applications at least thirty days prior to each deadline.

- Drafting and finalizing essays that reflect knowledge specific to self, goals, and schools.

- Maintaining a curious, courteous, and positive outlook when exploring schools, visiting campuses, and communicating with parents, teachers, counselors, and friends regarding admissions activities.

- Visiting schools after offers are received, and then taking into account learning style, curriculum, and course offerings, as well as other self-assessment factors when determining where you enroll.

You can and will soon complete all steps to admissions success. As you proceed, you will see that essay writing actions can also be defined and completed with ease. In fact, as the next chapter reveals, it is easy as ABC!

The best of times are truly ahead. This handbook will help you achieve your goal—chapter by chapter, application by application, and essay by essay.

Bridget Klenk

A college counselor and English teacher, Bridget is one of the contributors you will get to know as you progress through this book. She offers her overview of the admissions process:

The admissions process can be incredibly mystifying to those who have never ventured beyond the traditional tour and information session. When I mention that I once worked in admissions before switching to "the other side" as a college counselor, people suddenly take great interest in my past. Students and parents listen to the advice, believing I may actually know some grand secret. It is as if some believe that admissions officers are omniscient and omnipotent regarding applicants and applications.

People want to know all the secrets. Some want confirmation that involvement in the Latin program must be regarded more highly than involvement in the Robotics club. Others want to know the magical number of Advanced Placement courses that will assure admissions in a highly competitive college. And some want to know how to write that perfect essay. Their searches for secrets reveal many misapprehensions and much gratuitous anxiety.

Regardless of where you are in the college search and application process, it is essential that you understand that the admissions process is mostly art and only a bit of science, more qualitative than quantitative. I have reviewed thousands of applications, and I can assure you that subjective interpretations and a great deal of admissions officer intuition will play a key role in determining the fate of your application. Will your SATs weigh heavily? Will your sophomore-year grades be detrimental? Can your essay tip the scales in your favor? Can a great essay personalize your candidacy and make a difference?

The answers to the first three questions are, in order, "yes, no, and maybe." Critical to the focus of this book, the answer to the fourth question is "most definitely!" The most accurate and sincere response to all of these questions is, "You can overcome any potential negatives by being positive, taking control over the admissions process, thinking and acting strategically, and communicating your thoughts articulately in essays, supplemental pages, and correspondence."

If too much information leaves you dizzy and filled with dread, believing that the world of admissions is little more than an unyielding maze, do not lose hope. The good news is that you, the applicant, have a great deal of freedom to plan your own course of action. By understanding the general process of admissions, remaining positive, and taking one step at a time, you will feel more confident and in control.

Generally speaking, most colleges and universities are interested in five key aspects of the application, including:

- Your high school record/transcript
- Standardized test scores
- Essay and/or personal statement
- Letters of recommendation from teachers
- Extracurricular activities: anything you devote your time to outside of the classroom

Although variation does exist from school to school, most admissions officers will agree that the high school record is the single most important factor in the entire process. Schools are interested in the grades achieved in the classes you have taken, and in any trends such as an improvement in grades from freshman through senior year, or a change in the level of courses (for example, taking standard classes in the first half of high school, then switching to intermediate or honors classes). Did you challenge yourself with a demanding course of study? What courses did you take as a sophomore? How did you do immediately after that year? It is better to push yourself in more difficult courses, perhaps risking a lower grade, than it is to take easy classes and earn all A's. Students and parents often find this truth very difficult to believe, but I promise you, this one stands true—take the tougher class!

After reviewing the high school transcript, different schools will place different value on the remaining components. Some will place great credence on letters of recommendation while others may be more or less interested in your standardized test scores. As for the essay or personal statement, most college admissions professionals concur: "A great essay rarely makes up for a weak academic record, and a mediocre essay won't necessarily consign your application to the deny list. But, a great essay makes me focus on you for a critical period of time and, often, it generates my curiosity about your candidacy. It is often that quantity of time and quality of curiosity that can make the difference."

Too many students dedicate an inordinate amount of time to trying to decide what to write rather than devoting these hours to putting pen to paper. In the following chapters you will be inspired to write your essays. For some, writing will come easily and be finished easily. For others, it will involve more time, energy, and emotions. All will see that admissions essay writing can be completed most effectively, with diminished anxiety, by following a series of well-conceived steps. Procrastination yields nothing. Immediate action puts you in control.

Last, I do have some general words of wisdom for juniors:

• Start early! Take SATs, SAT IIs, and ACTs by the end of junior year.

• Self-reflect: Think about who you are and what is important to you. Ask yourself how, where, or if any of this will fit into finding a school that is the right match for you.

• Do your research: Read the college mail that will soon inundate you, visit schools' Web sites, establish a relationship with your college counselor (or whichever school official can help you with this process).

- Create a preliminary list of schools in which you may be interested.

- Schedule campus visits: Attend information sessions, take campus tours, and meet with admissions representatives.

- Become discerning: Begin to eliminate schools in which you no longer have interest.

- Continue to focus on your academics! Although the college search and application process quickly takes on a life of its own, do not let your grades slip or opt out of challenging classes. Junior year grades and classes are of great importance!

Though junior year can be critical, don't be too concerned if you are already a senior. I have worked with many students who complete most, if not all, of the admissions steps during the fall of their senior year. It makes things very exciting, and, clearly, a bit intense, but it can be done. No matter your age, nor where you are in the overall process, you can and will be successful. You will complete all steps to admissions success, including essay writing. I am very pleased that I will have the opportunity to motivate your efforts.—*BK*

Robert Massa

A veteran admissions professional who has reviewed thousands and thousands of applications and advised even more candidates, Robert offers a comprehensive overview:

The college admissions process taken as a whole may seem at best daunting, and at worst overwhelming. But broken into its component parts, it is manageable. We'll go into some of these in more depth later, but it is important now for you to know what composes the "big picture" and how the essay fits into the overall process. In general, admissions is best viewed and completed as a five-stage series of feelings, thoughts, and deeds.

Stage One: Identification

Gathering knowledge of yourself and knowledge of the schools you are interested in begins the process. But, don't limit initial efforts to introspection. Active exploration and research is required at all stages, especially the first one:

- Inventory your strengths and weaknesses, your learning style, and your style of interaction with others. Identify your educational objectives. Think of your favorite teacher, and why that person had an impact on you.
- Based on self-knowledge, identify some college characteristics that are important to you: size, location, majors, unique programs, university vs. college, and average SAT score and GPA of those admitted, for example. Think about whether you want to be at the top scores of those admitted, at the bottom, or somewhere in the middle.
- Use a search engine like *www.usnews.com* or *www.petersons.com* or printed reference books, which focus on parameters of most interest, to generate your initial list of potential schools.

Take this list to your counselor for analysis, discussion, and fine-tuning.

Stage Two: Discovery

Once you have a list that you and your counselor think is appropriate (at first there may be ten or twenty colleges on that list), begin to visit each Web site. Look for defining characteristics such as programs and how professors teach (lecture versus demonstration; fieldwork; research) to match your learning style. Look for evidence of student involvement in and out of class to coincide with your style of interaction. Use your Web research skills to explore beyond the admissions pages to department and faculty/student sites.

- Take notes along the way. Note your first impressions or questions in the margins of admissions publications, or on Post-it notes. Mark up viewbooks and brochures, as well as large reference books. ("Viewbooks" is the common phrase that admissions professionals use for their key publication. Web sites, brochures, and other admissions materials are also inspirational.) Don't concern yourself with rankings that seek to either quantify quality through numeric data or to rank schools based on unscientific samples of student ratings such as "the best school for community service" or "the best party school."

- Use a loose-leaf notebook with dividers to keep track of your observations. Also list college application and financial aid deadlines on the divider separating each college.

- Schedule some campus visits during the summer after your junior year. You may also do this during the spring break of your junior year, but only if you have completed the inventory during the identification stage. Remember that by visiting during the summer you gain only a partial sense of the place. Most students will want—if possible—to revisit their serious choices again in the fall or spring, when school is in session. Be sure to write down impressions in your loose-leaf notebook immediately after the visit. Otherwise, months later, all of the visits will blur.

- Schedule an interview if you can, giving the admissions counselor a chance to get to know you personally. Come prepared to speak about an issue you care about passionately. The interviewer might not let you talk about this, but it is best to be prepared. Use the interview to show the admissions person that you understand yourself and the college. Ask questions that demonstrate this level of understanding. Do not ask about things that you should already know, like student/faculty ratio and how many books are in the library.

Stage Three: Determining Target Schools

Using the information you have collected thus far, construct a grid of those factors that are important for you to consider, and rate each college subjectively on how it meets your criteria. Then review this grid with your parents and counselor for feedback and clarification.

- Don't worry too much about cost at this stage. You may go to the College Board's financial aid planner section (*www.college board.org*) to get a sense of your expected family contribution. Most colleges use a variation of this formula, and you can expect financial aid, which may make your attendance possible, to cover all or part of the difference between what your family is expected to contribute and what the college costs.
- Look for non-need academic scholarships and qualifications. If you fit the objective criteria, chances are that you will receive an award. If a college does not offer these awards and your family's contribution exceeds the price charged, it's likely that you will have to pay the full amount without any grant or scholarship assistance, though loans may still be available for you and your parents.
- Select six or seven schools that meet your criteria and that are appropriate with regard to academic qualifications. Many practitioners will advise that you have one or two "reach schools," two or three "likely schools," and at least one "sure bet" school. While there is some benefit from this, my experience tells me that applying to "reach schools" seldom yields positive results, no matter how solid you think you are. The most highly competitive schools have so many qualified applicants that most students will

need a "hook" to get in, such as a special talent, connection to a graduate, geographic or ethnic diversity, or extraordinary leadership. I encourage you to select six or seven "first-choice colleges"— any one of which you would be thrilled to attend if you are admitted and you can afford.

Stage Four: Preparing the Application

Once you have identified where you will apply, clarify how and when, and then do so. Focusing on your schools of choice required a great deal of effort and thought, yet you need to be energized for the tasks ahead. Paperwork may seem the most mundane of the steps involved, but filling out forms, forwarding transcripts and test scores, and following up on all supplemental materials is required for you to reach your ultimate goals. Do keep those goals in mind whenever you feel a bit overcome by details. Getting those "Congratulations, you're in" letters and e-mails will be an amazing achievement, well worth the effort.

- Be sure you are aware of deadlines and of required tests for each school. It is your responsibility to meet all requirements.
- If a college accepts the common application, use it. It is a myth that this somehow puts a candidate at a disadvantage. (As the title reveals, the common application is "one size fits all," and it includes essays. We'll talk more about this in Chapter 7.) Also, remember that many colleges accepting the common application will require you to complete a short supplement.
- Do not be afraid to include supplemental information, particularly about why you and specific schools are great matches. Show them you have done your homework.
- Ask several teachers to write letters of recommendation for you early. Rather than giving these teachers a resume to assist them in their writing, give them a list of what you discovered about yourself during the investigation process, and how each college fits

your characteristics. Ask the teacher to provide evidence of these characteristics from your classroom interaction/performance.

• Complete the essay according to the specific advice given in this book. The essay is just one part of this process. By following this advice, you will maximize the impact your writings can have on the overall admissions process.

• Mail your application well before the deadline. If I were applying to colleges knowing what I know now, I would clearly want mine to be among the first applications reviewed rather than the last. Waiting to the last minute increases the chances that some important piece of paper may not make it into your file at the time of the first read, or that something might be overlooked. You have to get these in eventually—so do it early!

Stage Five: Making the Choice

If you have approached this process in an organized way, the decision-making process at the end should, frankly, be difficult, because each college to which you have been admitted is appropriate and clearly a good choice.

• If possible, revisit each school to get a final sense of feel and fit. Stay overnight if you can, talk to students, sit in on classes, meet with faculty. How do you feel when visiting campus? Does any particular school seem intuitively better than the others?

• Re-examine so-called "placement and outcomes" data for each institution. What do their graduates do and how did their school help them get there? How many enroll in graduate or professional programs? How many get jobs right out of college, and where are these jobs? Speak with a career advisor directly to discuss these questions and to discuss the resources and services offered to facilitate students' maximizing their potential.

• If price is an issue, contact the financial aid office to find out if they will entertain what they call an appeal of your award.

Simply, this is a re-examination of the information you and your family submitted, and it is required to make any changes to the amount of need-based or merit-based funds that are offered. Take appropriate steps to maximize your award, including providing supplemental information regarding circumstances that may have changed since you first completed your application, but do not put financial aid professionals in the position of matching an award from another college.

- Discuss price versus value with your parents. This is something that should definitely be discussed with your family, especially if you are not paying all of your tuition.

- Do not make your final decision based on a college's ranking, its perceived prestige, or what your friends might say. This decision is one that will impact your life and, though it's not irreversible (you can always transfer if you discover later that your decision was wrong), you nevertheless want to select a college that will maximize your chances for the type of growth and development that will set you up for success in whatever you do after graduation.

In the end, even with all of this preparation, the decision can become an emotional one or one that is based upon your instinct. This is fine, especially if you were methodical and purposeful throughout the process. Just don't look back. Once you have made your decision, don't second-guess yourself. Revel in your decision, be confident that you've made the right choice.

The college admissions "market" is not as tight as the public is lead to believe from press accounts that most often focus on a few extremely selective colleges and universities. In fact, of the 2,400 four-year colleges and universities in the country, only about 130 or so admit fewer students than they turn down. Approaching the process logically, understanding that the criteria for selecting a college start and end with you, showing more concern about "fit" than "image," and being thorough during the process will yield satisfying results in the end. You will minimize the angst that so often occurs as well as the conflict between parents and their children that's inherent to this process. Go at it logically and honestly and you will be successful. Have fun (really), and good luck!—*RM*

Jordan Nadler

Concludes with a concise and insightful perspective:

Does the prospect of applying to college scare you? Does the idea of not knowing where you will spend the next four years make you a bit anxious? Or, better, are you very, very excited about the what lies ahead? I know, I know, it's scary or stressful for some, and anxiety-provoking or exhilarating for others. We're all different and we respond to common circumstances in different ways. If you're one of those "too good to be true" kids I never trusted in high school, you're amazing and already have a great attitude. If you're like me, a person who must add a little drama to almost any decision or situation, you'll do just as well. Remain positive and keep focused on the fact that in the end, everything will be fine. No matter who you are, or how you will respond emotionally to the intellectual and logistical steps of college admissions, I promise that you will be admitted to an amazing school and that you will have a great college career. Your overall admissions efforts and specific essay writing activities will most definitely end in success.

You can go to a school of any size, in any state, and choose it for a variety of reasons. The stress or positive anticipation of this decision will be with you until the end, but it is important to remember that your goal is to make the right decision for you, not for anyone else. As you progress, keep in mind that at some point, it will be very clear when you have found the right school. The application process is simply the means of getting you there. You will most definitely get there, and when you do, you will be very happy.

Think of the process as a complex and often trying, yet clearly identifiable series of events that can be thought of as addition and subtraction. Not everyone is a math wizard, but we all can relate to the pluses and minuses of math, the pros and cons of college admissions. Your test scores and GPA help guide you toward considering schools that are the best academic fit for you—you add schools that seem receptive to candidates with your academic strengths and test scores, and subtract those that are not.

Once you have a concentrated list, begin conducting some Web searches and talking to counselors, parents, friends, family members—anyone who will listen—about your choices. The more research you do, the more people you talk to, the better. Everyone is willing to help, and everyone has an opinion or two or more about each school you find appealing. To make sense of all the information you receive, no matter the source, you can create and use pros-and-cons listings, grids, folders, spreadsheets, and other variations on the compulsive note-taker and analyst themes. I don't want to tell you how I did my final list-making, but I warn you not to depend on memory, nor on your parents' memories. Some note-taking is advised.

Then, there is the college visit. When you are actually in each setting, gauge whether you can see yourself attending the institution you are considering. Honestly, you may not be able to put your finger on why campus visits impact your decisions and contribute to adding and subtracting names from your list, but, believe me, the campus visit is one of the most valuable things you can do during this process.

If a school feels right, trust that feeling, and forge ahead to the technical part of the process—completing an application. After that you'll be able to get to the most expressive part of this process—writing the essay.

Really, the essay can be the most enjoyable and hands-on aspect of the entire admissions and application process. The essay gives you a chance to go beyond addition and subtraction to multiplication. Once you have the bottom-line list of schools complete, the essay is your opportunity to multiply your chances of being admitted. This requested writing sample allows you to factor in your personality, values, and communication talents. And, in turn, it gives admissions officers the opportunity to recognize personality types and important "non-numerical intangibles" that they believe will fit with their institution's profile.

Your essay will not be graded, and there is no right answer, so by all means have fun with it. It sure beats standardized tests! Writing the essay will, if you read the rest of this book, be easy and, I hope, enjoyable. With great essays, you can apply to colleges and universities with confidence, knowing that the outcome will be positive and that your efforts will end in success. You will get into and enroll in a great school and have a great time as a student at that school. I did it. You can do it too.—*JN*

Now that you've gained a sense of what the overall admissions process is, it's time to focus on the best part. The admissions essay will be your literary masterpiece, your *Tale of Two Cities*.

The chapters that follow will share novel ideas for preparing, drafting, and editing essays. While some contributors have metaphorically compared admissions to a mathematical problem, making it as easy as adding one, two, and then three, you soon will see that essay writing is truly just a matter of knowing your ABCs.

2 | ABCs of Essay Writing
and Admissions Success

WHETHER YOU ATTRIBUTE the statement "Every journey begins with a single step" to an ancient and mystical Asian philosopher, to a fortune cookie, or to a bumper sticker, the fact remains that tasks thought of as difficult are best completed one step at a time. Your road map for the journey to essay writing success can be, and will be, easy to follow.

Now that you have completed the first chapter, you have a sense of what will be involved in the overall trip from applications through college admissions and enrollment. You can see the landscape of this grand journey, and you are prepared to navigate along its highways. Also, you now realize which part of this journey involves taking the essay writing road. You won't have to write down these directions, because they will be as easy as ABC. In fact, the six basic steps to essay writing can be quickly memorized using a cleverly presented (we hope) A through F step-by-step model.

The most important elements of essay writing include Assessment of personal characteristics and achievements, Brainstorming themes and topics, Choosing a topic or two, Drafting two essays, Editing both drafts, and Finalizing.

The six steps to essay writing success are the foundation upon which much of this book is built. After this chapter, we will support you through the initial steps and will give you the information you need to complete the process with minimum frustration and maximum potential. As you progress chapter by chapter, we will guide you on your journey to successful essay writing. The road won't always be perfectly smooth or straight, but you can avoid potholes and detours if you follow the tips and techniques presented.

Assessment of Personal Characteristics and Achievements

Too many people leap into essay writing before they look into "mirrors of self-knowledge." These essayists read topics and questions on applications and then quickly draft responses, presenting what they think essay readers will want to see. This "leap before you look" approach does not maximize the potential the writer has to create the self-expression pieces really sought by admissions professionals.

As we explained in Chapter 1, essays must be more than illustrations of writing style. They will be reflective of your dreams, perspectives, and capabilities. Truly, the best essays answer questions and themes posed while revealing a story that only you can tell. Admissions professionals definitely want to review documents that offer insight into your motivation and emotions. They want your writing to reveal core personal characteristics that cannot be reflected by your GPA and scores from college admissions examinations.

Self-assessment will include more than a simple listing of activities and achievements. Exercises in Chapter 3 will ask you to identify attitudes and values, as well as events and people that are most significant. "The Me That Others Don't Often See Inventory" will, through a series of creative questions, reveal information you can share in your essays. These questions will focus on key events, significant individuals, personal values, passions, and curiosities. They will bring to the surface the thoughts that might otherwise remain silent. This first step is very important. Don't skip to the next. You are getting closer and closer. Keep going one step at a time. Don't hesitate to take the next, but don't rush, either.

When you have answered these meaningful assessment queries, you will be ready for steps two through six.

Brainstorming Themes and Topics

This involves generating creative ideas spontaneously, without time for reflection. Many, many essayists stare at printed or online applications hoping that a voice from heaven might suddenly reveal strategies as well as answers. Most likely, the voices heard will be those of parents asking "Have you written anything yet?" Brainstorming, or freestyle thinking as others might call it, is crucial to the creative process. You can break free from the "What do they want to read?" and "What will get me in?" attitudes, and evolve to a "What do I want to reveal about myself?" perspective.

Brainstorming can be done simply and easily by quickly jotting down ideas in the margins of this book. Note your first reactions to school-specific questions and to the typical essay themes that appear in Chapter 8. Listing keywords you might include in these essays is a good getting-started approach. While it might seem strange, first say the words or phrases aloud, and then write them down. By doing so, you will overcome any inhibitions and be more spontaneous. Real essay writing should be thought of as enjoyable and creative, not as a necessary evil imposed upon you by admissions-office monsters. Approach your brainstorming with an enthusiastic "What do I want them to read" attitude.

Choosing a Topic or Two

We've already shown that it doesn't take a rocket scientist to understand admissions. So, choosing a topic or two does not require a highly skilled surgeon. Simply decide which topics will allow you to share the most with those who will read and rate your essays within specific frameworks of content, style, structure, and length.

The topics you choose cannot be thought of as belonging to admissions offices, nor as impersonal words appearing online or on paper. Application questions are most often so open-ended that you can respond to them in varied and creative ways. Essays must show that you understood the question, and that you were inspired by a particular theme, but there is no right answer to these questions. The "easiest essays" are those that inspire you most and don't stress you out, so you can share the most insightful answers.

Ultimately, your essays will become words illustrating feelings, ideas, and opinions. These snapshots of yourself must be clearly visible to readers and inspire positive evaluations of you as a writer and as a person. After sharing these words, you will be invited by readers to join their academic, cocurricular, and residential communities.

Choosing a topic can never be thought of as a chore or be imposed upon you by others. You are in charge of this critical step. Pick those that can easily inspire brainstorming and, next, help you begin the first draft. Choose with your heart as well as with your head. Feelings about essays are as important as ideas. You'll know which topics and questions are best for you. Remember, the essay is a way of sharing information about yourself. Be inspired, not intimidated, by the questions.

Drafting Two Essays

Drafting, for some, means "stream of consciousness" writing. For others, it means following guidelines regarding introductory, supporting, and concluding paragraphs. While brainstorming was encouraged as an important early step, focus gained from structure is suggested here.

Once you have identified topics of interest, outline each of the two essays. As simple as it sounds, admissions professionals want essays to have a beginning, middle, and an end. They do appreciate the traditional method of a hypothesis, supporting statements, and conclusion.

Many schools will ask you to complete a long and short essay. Of course, you will most likely be applying to more than one institution. Draft two essays. For the most part, you will be able to adapt these two essays to the requests of all the schools to which you are applying. As you progress, one essay might grow to be the one you like the best, and the one to use as your primary document.

You should now have lists of topics or themes highlighted in this handbook, jotted on paper, or saved as word-processor documents. These lists should include brainstormed notes or key phrases, as well. Outlining prior to drafting is a natural offshoot of these lists. An effective approach could involve:

- Identifying the concluding statement or revelation you will make in the final paragraph
- Noting the three or four key elements or key points that must be contained within the document
- Naming the story you wish to tell the reader
- Naming the introductory paragraph, the two to four supporting paragraphs, and the concluding paragraph, using phrases that best characterize what you want the reader to conclude from each
- Creating traditional Roman numeral or bullet-point outlines, citing key themes of each paragraph as well as subheadings of supporting and concluding paragraphs, and the sentences within each

Sample Outlines

Following are a few outlines that could have been used to create the Sample Two essay that appears in Chapter 8. The essay responds to this request: "You have just completed your 300-page autobiography. Please submit page 217." Outlining can be very structured or more freeform in style. No matter which approach you take, outlining is an important part of the brainstorming and drafting steps to essay writing. Be sure to review how these outlines were ultimately transformed into a finished admissions essay.

WORKING TITLE: NOMAD, NO HOME, NO PROBLEM
Key Themes
- Many homes, many moods
- Hanover, D.C., Princeton, Stockton, Pittsford
- Frustrations associated with transitions
- Confidence in the face of changing circumstances
- Coping with changes brought on by circumstances beyond one's control
- Varied past experiences, realities of the present, unknown future
- College transitions, attitudes, and goals
- Lessons learned, and applications to academics

WORKING TITLE: RELUCTANT NOMAD, ENTHUSIASTIC TRAVELER
Introductory Paragraph
- Many moves
- Reactions to each move
- Family
- Nesting

Supporting Paragraphs
- New Hampshire, D.C., New Jersey, California, New York
- Different cities, cultures, self
- Emotional challenges of moving
- Adjusting to change and insecurities
- Defining self by geography, psychology, or culture
- Lessons learned with each move

Concluding Paragraph
- Complaining to complacent
- Acceptance for growth
- Lessons learned and applied to the present and future
- Implications for college and beyond

WORKING TITLE: THE RELUCTANT NOMAD,
NO LONGER MAD AT DAD

   I. Paragraph One: Reluctant Nomad
- A. Different Cities and Different Houses
  1. Emotional and Logistical Consequences
  2. Adjustment
- B. Nesting

  II. Paragraph Two: Princeton to Stockton
- A. Different Lifestyle
- B. Adapting to New Surroundings
  1. Fitting In
  2. Adaptation
- C. New Home

 III. Paragraph Three: California Girl
- A. Defining Self as Californian
- B. Adapting Yet Fearing Future Consequences
  1. Fears Become Realities
  2. Search for Self

 IV. Paragraph Four: Stockton to Rochester
- A. New Place, New School
- B. New Self
  1. Similarities and Differences
  2. Lessons of Adjustment

  V. Paragraph Five: Moving Means Growing
- A. Values and Self
- B. Who I Am
  1. Adaptable
  2. Flexible

C. Just Along for the Ride
1. Adapting to College
2. Applying Lessons Learned to College

Another approach is to ask yourself the following questions, and then transform the answers into paragraph guidelines.

- What are the topics I most want to write about?
- For each topic, what three to five points do I wish to make?
- Do I have interesting anecdotes associated with either or both topics?
- What was the most surprising thing revealed by the self-assessment activities?
- Have I already written an essay or two that can be transformed into a great college admissions essay?

When creating drafts, do not be too concerned with word length or try to write the "perfect essay" on the first attempt. Initially, all you want to do is transform concepts, themes, and keywords into sentences and paragraphs that might appear in some semilogical order. Later, when editing, you will change order, rework content, and create the most effective finished products.

Editing Both Drafts

When you reach this stage, you have already drafted two separate essays. Each responds to specific questions or topics presented on applications. When drafting you were not concerned with length, but when editing, refer to "required" or "suggested" word totals. You won't get essays to desired lengths right away, but eventually less will be more, and the essays will be close to the goal word count.

During initial editing stages, think about tone. Are you trying to be serious, sincere, creative, humorous, light, or all of the above? Can you achieve your goals using a consistent tone? What is the most appropriate tone for you?

Next, focus on content and format, both of which are crucial to producing great essays. Do both of the works in progress have a sense of structure and balance? Do they introduce a theme, image, or opinion clearly at the beginning? Do supporting paragraphs flow from the introductory one, revealing more and more as the reader progresses? Is the concluding paragraph clear, concise, and, in some cases, surprising? Also pay very close attention to proper grammar and spelling. Do not rely on your computer's grammar and spelling checker; use a good style guide and dictionary instead.

Last, but not least, employ strategic thinking. Do essay drafts contain revelations or surprises? Do they share things about you directly, or through intriguing literary twists and turns? Does your essay contain school-specific content and references? If yes, why? Do you present themes appropriately?

Remember, by working on two essays you will eventually allow yourself choices. You will be prepared to adapt one or the other for schools requiring more than one essay. It is very, very rare that students create distinct essays for each school.

Finalizing

While you will continue to focus on tone, content, and format, at this stage you will be proofreading and fine-tuning the messages, metaphors, and imagery of both essays. In this last of the six steps to essay writing success, ask yourself the following questions:

- Does the essay share insights that are not obvious, even to those who know you?
- Does the essay have a clear focal point, conclusion, or revelation?
- Is every paragraph, sentence, or word necessary?
- Does it inspire the reader to ask questions about you, the author?
- Does it show commitment, passion, or dedication?

- Does the essay project you in sincere and clear ways?
- Is the work original? Does it present a traditional issue in an original way?
- Does the essay reveal things about you that may not be evident to someone who only read your application or reviewed your "brag sheet"?
- Does the essay show your feelings or values?

All responses to the previous questions should be "yes," "definitely," or "for sure!" Any "maybe," "don't know," or "not sure" answers indicate that you should go back to steps E or, if necessary, D. Most often some editing will do, but don't be afraid to start over, drafting a new document. Also, have one or two trusted individuals, including teachers, counselors, friends, and persons who attend or who have graduated from your school(s) of choice, read and react to your essay(s). Have a second set of eyes, as well as someone else's heart and head, review your drafts. Ask them to answer the questions in the previous list.

Give yourself the luxury of putting down the so-called "final drafts" prior to completing the real fine-tuning and finishing efforts. Don't allow deadlines to take control of or stifle your creativity. Just as the drafting and editing processes are best completed over a period of time, finalizing is best done patiently and calmly, without looking at the clock or calendar as a deadline quickly approaches. Start early to allow enough time for all of the six steps!

Now let's go all the way back to the beginning of the alphabet, and learn more about step A! Subsequent chapters will encourage you to complete the remaining five steps. Brainstorming, Choosing, Drafting, Editing, and Finalizing will be inspired as you review typical questions, examine sample essays, explore structure and style, and learn about editing and critiquing techniques.

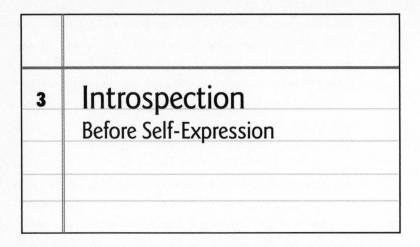

3 | **Introspection**
Before Self-Expression

BREAK OUT THE HIGHLIGHTERS. Put pen or pencil in hand. Click on "new document." You are now ready for immediate, creative, and critical action. Just a few pages ago, you learned the six steps to essay writing success. Do you remember our ABCs? Here they are again:

Assessment of personal characteristics and achievements, Brainstorming themes and topics, Choosing a topic or two, Drafting two essays, Editing both drafts, and Finalizing. These are the foundations upon which your essays will be built.

This chapter quickly and easily facilitates the first step. It will also give you information and inspiration needed to complete subsequent steps. As you progress through the ABCs, we will continue to reinforce the fact that your essays should not just be writing samples. To be effective, they will be expressions of self as well as ideas. Your wonderful essays will reveal thoughts and feelings, allowing readers insights into your personality and hidden perspectives. "The Me That Others Don't Often See Inventory" will, through a series of questions, reveal information you can share in essays. After you answer the questions, you will be ready for steps two through six. Warning: No matter how motivated and enthusiastic you are, and how eager you are to start writing, complete this critical first step. You can peek ahead and begin some brainstorming, but self-assessment is crucial. Believe it or not, it can be enjoyable as well as informative. Go for it!

After you complete the first Q&A exercise, progress to "The Institution Inspiration and Image Inventory." This exercise provides a framework for identifying interesting facts and important information related to schools of choice. Amazingly, too few essay writers utilize "viewbooks." Research is a critical part of any writing assignment. Reporters and authors always gather facts, figures, and background information prior to drafting any sort of document; unfortunately, college admissions essay writers rarely do so.

By identifying historical, mission-focused, curricular, and current-event issues related to schools of your choice, you will be inspired to brainstorm and, later, draft exceptional essays. You will be able to add strategic references that show you have done your homework and, most important, that you care about your target schools. Ultimately you will be able to determine how and when to incorporate such references into your essays, into cover pages, or into "any additional information" sections requested in applications.

The Me That Others Don't Often See questions will focus on key events, significant individuals, personal values, passions, and curiosities. They will bring to memory the thoughts that might otherwise remain dormant. After the exercise, you will be ready to incorporate some of the information into your writings. The Institution Inspiration and Image Inventory also bring to the surface ideas that might have otherwise not seen the written light of day.

Answers to questions in both exercises should be brief. Quick and concise responses are best. It's not important to offer complete sentences. Simply identify keywords and enter abbreviated phrases.

The first inventory exercise can be completed directly in the book, but before you do the second, please make a copy of the exercise or mark your answers on separate pages. This will allow you to complete the exercise again later, once you have truly targeted schools.

The Me That Others Don't Often See Inventory ✎

1. Who are the two individuals who have most influenced you in your life to date?

   _____

   _____

   How have these two individuals influenced you?

   _____

   _____

   _____

   _____

   _____

2. Who are the two individuals who most influenced you academically?

   _____

   _____

   How have these two individuals influenced you?

   _____

   _____

   _____

   _____

   _____

   _____

   _____

3. What five words would these individuals who have influenced you use to describe you?

_____

_____

4. Who are the two individuals who truly know you the best?

_____

_____

How would they describe you?

_____

_____

_____

_____

_____

Is there something about yourself that you have never revealed to these individuals? If so, what?

_____

_____

_____

_____

_____

5. What five words would you use to describe yourself?

_____

Why did you select these words?

_____

_____

_____

_____

_____

Which two words that you chose would most surprise friends and family?

_____

_____

_____

_____

_____

_____

6. What two meaningful and memorable experiences have most impacted how you think or feel?

_____

_____

Who was involved in these experiences, and what were their roles?

_____

_____

_____

_____

_____

_____

How did these experiences change or solidify your views or feelings?

_____

_____

_____

_____

_____

_____

_____

7. What are the two most important lessons you have learned about life?

   _____

   _____

   Who was involved in teaching you those lessons, and what were their roles?

   _____

   _____

   _____

   _____

   With whom would you like to share these lessons?

   _____

   _____

   _____

   _____

8. What are two lessons you learned as a result of adversity or failure?

   _____

   _____

   Who was involved in these lessons, and what were their roles?

   _____

   _____

   _____

   _____

   _____

   _____

   _____

With whom would you like to share these lessons?

_____

_____

_____

9. Who are two living individuals you would like to meet?

_____

_____

How would you describe yourself to these individuals before your meeting?

_____

_____

_____

_____

_____

_____

10. Who are two historical or fictional individuals you would like to meet?

_____

_____

How would you describe yourself to these individuals before your meeting?

_____

_____

_____

_____

_____

_____

11. What are your two greatest academic successes? Think about essays, projects, or classes in which you achieved honors or superior grades; those of which you were most proud.

    _____

    _____

    Who was involved in these successes, and what were their roles?

    _____

    _____

    _____

    _____

    Who doesn't know about these successes, but should know?

    _____

    _____

    _____

    _____

12. What are your two best accomplishments so far?

    _____

    _____

    Who was involved in these accomplishments, and what were their roles?

    _____

    _____

    _____

    _____

    _____

    _____

    _____

Who doesn't know about these accomplishments, but should?

_____

_____

_____

_____

13. What five activities do you like the most, and why?

_____

_____

_____

_____

_____

14. What five activities do you like the least, and why?

_____

_____

_____

_____

_____

15. What skills and perspectives have you gained from your education to date? Think about significant class projects, activities, summer programs, special courses, or academic honors and broad, not subject-specific, skills and lessons you learned from each.

_____

_____

_____

_____

_____

16. Why do you, personally, want to go to college?

_____

_____

_____

_____

_____

_____

_____

_____

17. What are your three favorite academic subjects?

_____

_____

_____

18. What are your three favorite cocurricular or social activities?

_____

_____

_____

19. What two recent events impacted you emotionally?

_____

_____

_____

_____

_____

_____

Who was involved in these events, and what were their roles?

_____

_____

_____

_____

Who doesn't know about these events, but should?

_____

_____

_____

_____

What specific emotions were generated by these events?

_____

_____

_____

_____

_____

20. Which three colleges or universities seem ideal to you?

_____

_____

_____

_____

_____

What about each school makes it attractive?

_____

_____

_____

_____

That wasn't so bad, was it? You now have a collection of ideas for when you brainstorm topics and when you begin to draft essays. If tempted, and you wish a preview of things to come, do look ahead! Turn to Chapter 8 and review typical topics presented. Surprise! Some questions posed on actual applications are identical to those in this list. Others are such that you can use information you wrote down here to begin brainstorming and drafting your essay.

Here's a bigger surprise! Look back at your answers to question 4, "Who are the two individuals who truly know you the best?" Please photocopy the following exercise and ask each person to complete the questions. Also, if they are not among those you listed, give a copy to your parents. Explain that you are trying to inspire yourself for college admissions essay writing. They'll be happy to participate. This activity will direct energy, anxiety, and emotion in a positive undertaking. Try to get parents, friends, and mentors involved with this exercise. Ask that they be as honest and creative as possible. No one should fret about how to answer these questions. Everyone should enjoy and have fun with this experience. Be sure not to give them too much time to think about each answer. Spontaneous responses are the best!

The Me That Others Most Often See Inventory

1. What five words would you use to describe the essay writer?

_____

_____

_____

_____

_____

Why did you select each word?

_____

_____

_____

_____

_____

Which two words would most surprise the essayist?

_____

_____

_____

_____

_____

2. Who are two individuals who you think truly know the essay writer the best?

_____

_____

How would these two people describe the essayist?

_____

_____

_____

_____

_____

3. What is one meaningful experience that you shared with the essayist that you remember most?

_____

_____

Who was involved in this experience, and what were their roles?

_____

_____

_____

_____

_____

How did these experiences change or solidify your views or feelings about the essay writer?

_____
_____
_____
_____
_____
_____

How would you have described the essayist to these individuals before their meeting?

_____
_____
_____
_____
_____
_____
_____
_____
_____
_____

4. What are the essay writer's two greatest accomplishments?

_____
_____

Who was involved in these accomplishments, and what were their roles?

_____
_____
_____

Who doesn't know about these accomplishments, but should?

_____

_____

_____

_____

_____

5. What five activities do you think the essay writer likes the most?

_____

_____

_____

_____

_____

6. What five activities do you think the essay writer likes the least?

_____

_____

_____

_____

_____

7. What three career-related dreams can you envision for the essay writer?

_____

_____

_____

_____

_____

_____

_____

8. Using twenty-five words or fewer, how would you describe the essayist academically?

_____

_____

_____

_____

_____

_____

_____

_____

If you had more words, what would you add?

_____

_____

_____

_____

9. What is it about college that you anticipate will be the essay writer's greatest first-year challenge?

_____

_____

_____

_____

_____

_____

10. What three colleges or universities seem ideal for this applicant?

_____

_____

_____

_____

_____

_____

Now, review responses to the final three questions of The Me That Others Don't Often See Inventory and The Me That Others Most Often See Inventory. The perspectives of others, often different from your views of self, can provide interesting insights and inspire essay writing.

Next, answer the following school-focused queries for three of your possible target schools. While you can do this for as many schools as you wish, at first focus on the three. Because you may not have focused on specific schools you are applying to, it's best to photocopy the questions or mark responses on separate pages. When you identify the schools you are definitely going to target, you will be able to complete this exercise again prior to beginning your essay writing.

The Institution Inspiration and Image Inventory provides a framework for identifying interesting facts and perspectives related to schools. Historical facts, mission statements, curriculum, student life, and current-event issues related to schools will support brainstorming and, later, support drafting efforts. Don't be concerned if you cannot answer all of the questions in this inventory on your first try. If you wish, give copies of the exercise to parents and others who may have accompanied you on campus visits or who have also reviewed any school literature. You should know from answers to The Me That Others Most Often See Inventory that the insights of others can be inspirational. Go for it. See what the others have to say.

Again, before you complete The Institution Inspiration and Image Inventory, please photocopy this particular exercise. When you do narrow down your choices, answer these queries for all target schools. Then, if you wish, you will be able to add essay references that show you have done your homework and that you can connect your values and goals to those of the schools you are applying to.

The Institution Inspiration and Image Inventory ✎

1. What are the three schools that most interest you today?

_____

_____

_____

_____

2. How many undergraduates attend each school, how many are there in each freshman class, and do you consider each school to be "small," "medium," or "large"?

_____

_____

_____

_____

3. Would you describe each school as "college," "university," or "something different"?

_____

_____

_____

_____

_____

_____

4. Who do you know who has attended or who is attending each of these schools?

_____

_____

_____

_____

_____

_____

5. What is the motto of each school and the stated mission of each school?

_____

_____

_____

_____

6. Would you describe each institution as "urban," "suburban," "rural," or "eclectic"?

_____

_____

_____

_____

7. What was a key phrase appearing in each school's viewbook, Web site, or other admissions documents that most appealed to you?

_____

_____

_____

_____

8. What other phrases appearing in each school's viewbook, Web site, or admissions documents appealed to you?

_____

_____

9. Who are two famous individuals who attended each of these schools?

_____

_____

_____

_____

10. Are the required courses or curriculum requirements of each school easy to identify, and can you note them in simple terms?

_____

_____

_____

_____

11. If you have reviewed printed or online editions, what headlines appearing in each of these school's daily or weekly student newspapers most intrigued you?

_____

_____

_____

_____

12. If you have visited any or all of these schools, what were the themes presented by comments of admissions professionals, tour guides, and others?

_____

_____

_____

_____

13. If you have visited any or all of these schools, what were your first impressions of the people you met—specifically, the students?

_____

_____

_____

_____

_____

_____

14. If you have visited any or all of these schools, what were the best questions you heard asked by anyone during your visit, and what were the answers to these queries?

_____

_____

_____

_____

_____

_____

15. If you could visit only one of these schools again, which one would you choose, and why?

_____

_____

_____

_____

16. How many "hits" did each school's name generate when you did an Internet search, and which hit seemed to provide the most intriguing information about each school?

_____

_____

_____

_____

_____

What do you think? As you quickly review your answers and those of others who completed these exercises, are you surprised, or not? Are new perspectives revealed or existing ideas reinforced?

Now that you have done the pre–essay writing inventories, you may feel ready to brainstorm topics. Because some important information must be addressed before you start brainstorming, it's a good idea to wait a bit. Until then, keep all responses to these inventories in a folder or binder. All essay writing documentation should be easily accessible. Also, if you are using a computer, create backups and, without being too paranoid or secret-agent-like, send yourself regular e-mails, attaching drafts and other documentation. This will ensure that no matter what happens, you will be able to access recent drafts in order to edit and finalize all documents. "The dog ate my paper" is no longer an acceptable excuse. Take steps to avoid "the disk drive ate my disk" circumstances as well.

You are doing great! Keep reading, moving forward page by page, chapter by chapter, closer and closer to great essays!

4 From Confusion
to Common Voice

AS THE PARABLE IS TOLD, a number of disciples once asked Buddha to determine who of the clerics were true believers and who shared false information regarding eternity, life, and man's relationship to nature. Rather than answer directly, Buddha shared an intriguing story about a raja, some blind men, and an elephant. It seems the raja once ordered that the blind men be asked to describe the elephant, a creature he assumed commonly perceived by all. The blind man who presented the head pronounced the elephant to be like a huge round pot. The one who felt the ear described the creature to be like a large flat leaf. The one who was given the trunk said the elephant was like a very thick rope, and the one who felt the tail said it was like a brush. After each described the elephant differently, the blind men began to argue and, ultimately, they came to blows.

Upon completing this story, responding to the puzzled faces of his disciples, Buddha shared the moral of this elephant tale: "As those touching various parts of the elephant, so are some clerics and disciples holding various views, blind and unseeing, yet believing they are all-knowing. With narrow views, they are quarrelsome and argumentative. To answer who is right and wrong, one must open ones eyes and heart, to see, hear, or feel many perspectives."

Though most people are not scholars contemplating the spiritual nature of our existence, it is still often valuable to gain knowledge of an issue from many sides—but with eyes wide open. By strategy, style, and content, this book presents diverse views of the elephant we call "admissions essay writing." Each collaborator presents personalized perspectives as well as advice on essay writing. Ultimately, through a common view that focuses on you, we will inspire drafting, editing, and finalizing and help you to open your eyes and perceive the most productive view as you progress.

I have learned many things from college counselors and admissions colleagues through my duties as a career services professional, advisor, and college administrator. One of the most important things I have learned is that techniques used to teach resume and cover letter writing, interviewing, and job search strategy can apply to admissions essay writing. The key to job search success is being able to visualize and then articulate goals via written documents (resumes, cover letters, and other communiqués) and in verbal circumstances (interviews). You project knowledge of yourself and of the job to those making decisions regarding interviews and offers. The better you present knowledge of yourself, the more likely you are to receive interview invitations and job offers.

The key to admissions essay writing is very much the same. You must carefully and creatively blend self-knowledge with awareness of educational goals, and, often, with knowledge of a particular institution. Over the years I have identified and taught basics of job search and resume writing. In Adams Media's *The Everything® Resume Book, 2nd Edition,* I list these steps to job search success: Set and articulate goals; create or update resumes; develop a target list of employers and a network of advocates; respond to posted openings; call to identify appropriate contacts, then fax, e-mail and mail resumes, cover letters and supporting materials; follow up, assess strategies, and enhance competencies; interview;

and finally receive and accept offers. In this way, a process too often perceived as complex is defined as a series of simple action steps.

Admissions essay writing involves similar actions. Essayists must set and effectively articulate goals via well-crafted documents. You must keep in mind your target readers, as well as desired outcomes, and utilize advocates to support your efforts. Through a series of initial and subsequent steps, you will fine-tune your message in order to succeed.

In *The Everything® Resume Book, 2nd Edition*, I also present seven steps to resume writing: Review samples; determine format, content, and order of importance; identify objectives and target audiences; inventory qualifications and achievements; analyze competencies and capabilities; draft and critique your resume; and, last, duplicate and distribute it. Readers of that book (which also contains sample resumes used for college admissions) are asked to follow these clear and concise steps in order to create specialized documents.

It is no coincidence that you can review and follow word-for-word the seven steps to resume writing to effectively complete admissions essays. Read these seven steps again and think about how they can apply to your essay writing efforts.

Resumes and admissions essays are both documents that inspire reviewers to think positively of writers and, ideally, to extend interview invitations and, ultimately, offers. Therefore, from the perspective of a career services professional who is often called the "resume doctor" or "job search coach," I urge admissions essay writers to:

• **Review samples:** Look over samples appearing in this book to gain inspiration and to learn to recognize the elements common to all good essays. Keep in mind that if others can create great essays, so can you!

- **Determine format, content, and order of importance:** Think about and follow general guidelines for essay structure and content, as well as the impact that order of presentation and personal revelation can have.

- **Identify objectives and target audiences:** Prior to drafting and, most definitely, during final editing stages, make sure that your essay is focused and written to specific readers, and that it addresses specific issues and facilitates desired outcomes (being offered admissions to specific schools).

- **Inventory qualifications and achievements:** Conduct self-assessment prior to drafting in order to identify your qualifications for admissions. Also note the achievements that reveal your potential for future success.

- **Analyze competencies and capabilities:** Include evaluations of your strengths as well as your potential and ambitions.

- **Draft and critique:** Write initial drafts, edit, then fine-tune your essays, always focusing on the power of editing and on content that can be inserted in essays to make them school-specific.

- **Duplicate and distribute:** Create individualized essays and submit them with all required and supplemental materials, including "additional information" statements.

As the father of a daughter who now attends college, I observed and, whenever possible, supported overall application actions and admissions essay writing, but only when given permission to do so. My daughter, as readers know by now, is a strong, well-spoken, and assertive individual. Her academic background, full of challenges, rewards, and recognitions, inspired confidence and motivated her to begin and complete admissions essay writing "on her own." In truth, she first did so as an assignment for an AP English teacher and she did have the support and guidance of others as she progressed. Objectively, I knew that she really didn't need my assistance, but subjectively, I so very much wanted to help. In reality, I did try to offer advice whenever I could, but Jordan was smart enough to decline in most cases, in very diplomatic ways.

Looking back, I recall some key issues and moments of heightened anxiety (for all), times when I really wanted to help (but was not invited to do so), and times when some of my suggestions were nixed (and appropriately so). Ideally, Jordan would have had a person or publication that would have been her "highest authority," providing much-needed emotional reinforcement as well as logistical advice.

I knew that Jordan was a good writer and that the long and short essays she drafted, revised, and finalized were well crafted, but she didn't really know how much to emotionally invest in these documents. As I listened to her concerns from a safe distance, it was clear to me that rejection would be worse if she thought that she had written and submitted "the very best." No matter how often I or others shared positive words, our advice did not easily translate to confidence during the essay writing phase of admissions for Jordan. The actual actions and thought associated with essay writing came easily to her, but the fears and anxieties associated with the overall admissions process did take their toll.

Many, if not most, essayists share fears and concerns like Jordan's. You, the essay writer, might overexaggerate the impact that these works will have on your application, placing undue pressure on yourself and on your writing. Remember, the essay is only one piece of the entire application, and it should be the one part that is most fun to do and the most creative! It should be the piece that is reflective of the person you know best—yourself. In truth, while the essay is reviewed, evaluated, and often "scored," it is not graded. It is not a final exam, nor a pass-fail indication of your life's achievements. Others will not judge it as harshly as you might imagine or fear. Admissions professionals just want to learn things about you that test scores and grades cannot provide.

Most parents just want their children to do their best. Some mistakenly encourage their kids to "write the perfect essay that will get you admitted to your first-choice school," causing more harm than good. These moms and dads, driven by the best of intentions and by the desire to help you avoid rejection, often react to essay writing in pressure-provoking and anxiety-heightening ways. If you think you are being pressured—and remember, you are in an emotionally heightened and perhaps overly sensitive state—be kind and thoughtful. Avoid confrontation; instead, seek inspiration. Offer Mom and Dad something constructive to do, like completing a self-assessment exercise. Do let them read your final version, but feel comfortable declining their offers to review earlier drafts. Let them know that you do want their feedback, but remind them that you are being supported by individuals (including counselors and teachers) and publications (like this one), and that it must be your essay, not theirs.

As the father of an admissions essay writer I encourage essayists to:

- Remain positive with yourself, with your peers, and with your parents, for you will be admitted to and enroll in a great school and have a terrific collegiate experience.
- Find an advocate or confidante, with whom you feel comfortable sharing anxieties, but don't dwell on the negative or get caught in a perpetual whining mode.
- Encourage the involvement of parents early in the process, specifically during the assessment phase, and have fun with their contributions.
- Ask your mom, dad, grandma, grandpa, uncles, aunts, and siblings for feedback when conducting self-assessment.
- Listen to the advice of others, and then, if you wish, in diplomatic ways—never be demeaning or deceptive—choose to ignore it covertly. Avoid overt confrontations.

• Realize that it is a sign of intellectual strength, not of weakness, to ask for help when needed.

• Remember that "when I applied to college" (a phrase that often precedes parental pearls of wisdom, and is too often responded to with disdain), was not that long ago, and that sometimes reflections of the past can inspire positive actions focusing on your future.

Yes, parents can inadvertently enhance, rather than diminish essay writing and overall admissions anxieties. Supportive parents accompany students on visits, ask what they believe are pertinent questions, and try to inspire conversations that will allow students to differentiate one school from another. Sadly, and often, their actions are responded to by "elbow in the ribs" reflexes of applicants, by "Oh, Dad" or "Oh, Mom" embarrassed sighs, or with verbal sparring during the drive home or to the next school. While I am not advocating a twisted version of a Victorian adage—"parents should be seen and not heard"—I do encourage parents to be as passive and thoughtful as possible and to utilize active listening skills rather than assertive and well-honed "telling" talents.

In Appendix 2, parents and applicants are offered insightful questions to ask during campus visits and after acceptance, as well as strategies for making a decision. For now, as a father and a counselor, I request that parents of essayists:

• Accept "no thank you" as an appropriate response to your offers to assist.

• Invest as much time, energy, and finances as you can in on-campus visits, for they will truly inspire essay writing and decision-making.

• Communicate any concerns with teachers or counselors, not necessarily directly with your son or daughter.

- If you really want to ask questions of your son or daughter, do so, but definitely listen to the answers without revealing your views or concerns.
- Be a great listener, not necessarily an advisor.
- Do have fun with assessment exercises and seek to inspire essay writing with anecdotes and funny stories introduced with "remember when."
- Avoid starting any statements with "you should . . . "

Jordan's views

on admissions essay writing:

As someone who recently wrote various college admissions essays, I will tell all of you who are just beginning the process to first relax. Yes, I said "r–e–l–a–x!" I know that is easy to say, but hard for many of you to do. The admissions essay seems like the most important piece of writing you have ever done. You may feel that the weight attached to its success is huge, pressing heavily on your shoulders and your heart. I know I did. But now, looking back, I realize that these essays are really only a small piece of the admissions puzzle and, honestly, that you have probably already written many amazing essays that were evaluated by teachers who are tougher than any admissions counselor.

Relax, because you have already succeeded in many arenas. Your life achievements as a mass, including courses and grades, extracurricular activities, community involvements, and family experiences, are the real big picture. Don't forget that. Once you understand that your essay will naturally arise from past lessons learned, from past successes as well as past challenges, you should allow yourself to relax. You have already succeeded, you have already lived your essay, and you have definitely shown others that you can achieve in an academic setting. Also, when you understand that your essay can only help you, and that it cannot hurt you, you can sit back and begin to write your essay. I think I heard once that procrastination is diminished by relaxation, so go for it!

Also, as noted earlier in this book, you might have already written your admissions essay. I used a large portion of an essay I wrote for a junior year English assignment for my admissions essay. Granted, it was no small coincidence that our teacher had assigned us a reflective personal essay, mid-March of our junior year, but still, for me psychologically, it was just another assignment. The pressure of thinking that colleges would be reading this piece of writing did not weigh on me when I actually sat down to write the first draft, when I edited it, or when I handed it in to one of my favorite teachers. Without a doubt, this meant a much calmer me. Truthfully, I may have been a little stressed (or, very stressed) when I sought to adapt this piece for applications, but in hindsight, I now realize that when I was most relaxed, I did my best and created a very good essay.

Don't stress if you can't think of a piece you've already written to use for your college applications. We have already given you plenty of ideas on how to get started on your essay, and you will receive many, many more sources of inspiration.

I can't emphasize enough that you should allow yourself plenty of time. No one wants to spend all of their winter vacation cooped up writing admissions essays. Leave time for revisions and, if needed, time to start over if after initial drafts you don't like your piece. The stress associated with preparation and writing of the admissions essay is enough without adding the pressures of time constraints. I have many friends who tell me that they work better twenty-four hours before an assignment is due. They proudly state that they work best under pressure. Well, I can't work that way, and I don't think most students work best that way. While the clock ticks with great regularity and predictability, due dates seem to sneak up on those who wait and those who have a lot to do.

Last, I would say get as many people to read your essays as possible, and listen to their critiques with a careful ear and an open mind. You don't want the admissions readers to be distracted by silly grammatical errors. Fresh eyes are needed to pick up on any typos. Once grammatical issues have been resolved, ask those who read your draft to look for content and format irregularities. Even though criticism is sometimes hard to take, it's worth hearing from others rather than letting your mistakes be revealed to college admissions officials. Those you trust, and those who care about you, will be honest. Some of their comments will yield changes, but many will not. Remember, it's your name on the application and on the essay. You get the final say on this writing assignment.

Summarizing, from my student-focused perspective:

- For piece of mind, in some way list all of your accomplishments, and remember that you have already written great essays.
- Reflect on a time when you wrote an essay that you liked and that a teacher liked, and remember how you did this task without unnecessary stress.
- Identify and think about adapting one of the essays you have already written.
- Write your admissions essays in the same way you have written so many other essays in the past, using the style and steps that yielded success.
- If you write using stream of consciousness first, do it. If you create detailed outlines, do it. If you write a thesis sentence and the introductory sentence for all other paragraphs first, do it. Whatever you've done before to write a great essay, do it again, now!
- Give yourself enough time to do your best, even if you have pulled all-nighters at the last minute to write "A papers" in the past.

- Allow trusted teachers, counselors, and others to read your finished essay, as if it is a draft, relying on their feedback for grammar, content, and format corrections and suggestions.
- Relax, because you will write a great essay and you will get into a great school.—*JN*

Bridget's multiple perspectives:

As a college counselor at a small independent school, I have had the privilege of reading hundreds of college essays. I've seen drafts in rough stages as well as drafts ready to be sent to schools. Helping applicants create an essay that best presents his or her voice, succinctly yet thoroughly, is truly challenging and rewarding. I struggle when guiding a student through the writing process. Ultimately, the final submission must accurately and honestly represent the student's thoughts and writing style, not that of a teacher, parents, friends, or, dare I say it, a counselor.

Essays must be written by the student and for the student. They cannot be contrived pieces written for the sole purpose of impressing admissions officers. Although students should seek the input of others when creating these important compositions, the final submission should not take on a contrived voice, distant from that of the original author. Your essays must, in all cases, be your work, creations that show your word craftsmanship as well as your personality. Counselors can inspire and critique, but you must compose and reveal your thoughts and feelings.

When I first read a student's essay, I expect that it has already undergone extensive "tweaking." I presume that the student is not showing me an initial draft representing stream of consciousness writing, but a piece that was written and rewritten a number of times. By sharing this assumption regularly and clearly, I am assured that the student has already devoted serious thought and effort to the essay. With well-organized thoughts down on paper, we focus on the mechanics and organization of the essay. At this point, an insipid essay can be given zing, and, conversely, the maudlin essay, more appropriate for daytime drama, can be cleansed and condensed. When students submit "critique ready" essays for my review, after they have used the essay writing lessons learned in English and other classes, I can best inspire essayists to ultimately create a personal and self-revealing piece.

To all admissions essay writers, I offer the following college counselor's suggestions for crafting an essay that represents you:

- Keep in mind what your application already says about your high school experiences, so that the essay will provide new information and perspectives.
- Think of this as an opportunity to write your own letter of recommendation. What would you want an admissions officer to know about you?
- Do not write what you think the admissions committee wants to hear. Rather, use your own active voice and write in your own style, revealing who you are as a person. Your topic does not need to be as unique as your approach for writing the essay and your ideas.
- Think small and do not ramble. All too often students try to cram too much into their essay. It is better to focus on one specific issue, event, or moment in time, clearly illustrating the nuances of your story.
- Do not use an artificial voice, flowery language, or unnecessary vocabulary.
- Remember, the technical aspects of your writing do count! Double-check your grammar and spelling and do not rely solely on the spell-check tools on your computer. Proofread your work!

- Follow the directions and adhere to the guidelines given. If the college requests that you write the essay in your own handwriting, do so. If they ask you to write "in the space provided" or give a specific length requirement, be sure to follow their requests.
- Make sure the thoughts in your essay are well organized.
- Provide a clean, printed copy of your essay for each application. Do not use photocopies.
- Put your full name and social security number on every page of your essay.
- Do not procrastinate! Many colleges make their essay questions available online over the summer. Go to some different Web sites for sample questions and write at least a draft of your personal statement. You should have written several drafts of your work before Thanksgiving.

In my role as an English teacher, my approach to teaching and grading general essays and admissions essays is quite different from the approach I have when mentoring students as a college counselor. In the classroom, it is essential that students understand and embrace the process of writing. I always begin at a fundamental level, devoting a significant amount of time to writing and stressing the importance of recognizing how you become inspired to write. Often this comes from reading the works of great authors. In addition, I encourage discussions about what is happening in students' lives, nourishing creative notions. You know that typical teacher statement: You should always focus on writing about topics important to you. Think and write about your passions. This is critical when approaching your college essay.

For the admissions essay you may be inspired by questions posed by others, but you will write about what you know best: yourself. You will avoid lofty, detached writing that is of little interest to anyone. Once you have identified various topics from those offered by each school, you should:

- Write for ten minutes (without pausing) on one or more topics, putting on paper the first thoughts that come to mind.
- Look at your writing, ask yourself why you chose this particular topic, seek to identify patterns to your writing, and begin informal outlining.
- Underline certain words, phrases, and/or sentences that represent key thoughts that have the potential to develop into thesis statements. Or, underline key elements of a formal and structured admissions essay.
- Write all of the underlined words, phrases, and sentences on a blank sheet of paper.
- Review this page and begin to cluster your thoughts by circling, highlighting, or drawing lines, making figurative and actual connections between like ideas.
- Identify one, two, or three ideas that you would like to develop further.
- If you find something that sparks your interest, begin to develop a formal essay, starting with an outline.
- If this exercise does not result in one or many topics from which to launch your writing, start again.
- Once creative brainstorming has revealed topics and potential logical components, follow traditional rules of essay writing, utilizing introductory, supporting, and concluding paragraphs as well as introductory, supporting, and transition sentences.
- Do not be discouraged if ideas do not flow immediately. Writing is hard work, and good writing rarely comes without a certain degree of struggle.

- Approach admissions essay writing as an evolving process, rather than anticipating that you will write your essay in an evening's time.
- Have confidence that you will produce a piece that best represents you as a unique individual and conveys a voice that is distinctively yours.

During my tenure as an admissions officer I read thousands of essays, most of which, I must confess, I don't remember. However, I do still recall one of the very first essays I ever read in my early days at the University of Rochester.

Although this very essay nearly cost me my job and could have resulted in a premature end to my admissions career, I share this embarrassing tale to inspire your essay writing. The author of this particular essay wrote about her favorite little eatery. She creatively drew connections between herself and this "greasy spoon" diner, illustrating a vivid literary portrait of who she was as a person, what was important to her, and how these qualities would transfer from her small, rural southern town to complement our urban campus in upstate New York. To most, a greasy diner in a sleepy town does not seem a striking topic for an admissions essay, yet it worked. It worked because it was quirky and original—just like this particular student. The essay was well written and crafted in such a way that I gained a clear image of her as a student and as a person. In fact, it worked so well that I picked up the phone and called this student, telling her just how much I enjoyed her essay. But, I had yet to review her transcript, her test scores, or any of the other significant information used when evaluating a student's application for admissions. Can you anticipate where the embarrassment and controversy might arise?

Although the tale had a happy ending with the student's academic record mirroring her sterling writing sample, an essay alone, regardless of how well it is written, is generally not enough to merit a student admission. In this particular instance the student was admitted, but our application review coordinator quickly informed me of the dreadful outcome that could have resulted. It would have been difficult to deny a student who I loudly lauded as an outstanding writer! Though I learned my lesson quickly, there still were one or two additional times in the years ahead when I wished I could once again pick up the phone and commend a student on an exceptionally well-written essay. Each of these pieces contained essential common qualities:

- They were honest and sincere, depicting a literary portrait of the writer as a person and as a student.
- They convinced me that the essayist was capable of meeting or exceeding the writing standards of our university.
- They captured my attention because of the essayist's obvious passion about the topic.
- When reading, they kept me wanting more; when finished, I wanted to read another piece written by this person.
- They convinced me that this was someone who would complement and enhance our community.—*BK*

Bob McCullough

For this chapter, we add the comments of another admissions professional. Bob McCullough is the associate director of admissions at Case Western Reserve University in Cleveland, Ohio. His areas of expertise include publications and recruitment technology, and his geographic focus spans California, Michigan, Oregon, Washington, and Ohio.

As an experienced admissions professional, I advise that you think of the application, specifically the essay, as your first college assignment. On one level, you want to do good work, impressing your professor with your intellect and range of expertise. Most simply, at a base level, you want to submit a finished product that is polished and thorough. When you're prompted for specific information, don't just blow it off as unimportant and then submit whatever you wish. As one of my mentors used to say, "The college application is a highly evolved document—each question has a purpose, and a shoddily prepared application not only fails to serve the purpose, it reflects poorly on you as an applicant, as a student, and as a person."

After the essay is submitted and you are admitted, you can extend the "college assignment" metaphor to the broader context of your college search and, ultimately, selection. Your assignment, should you choose to accept it, is to find the School That Ultimately Fits, Fast. So, if you want to use a creative acronym, you will soon seek "the right STUFF." The question of how to find a school that ultimately fits, and how you can find it fast, is addressed in Appendix 2. But for now, remember to always start your essay writing thinking that you have the right stuff, and that you will demonstrate your attributes in the essay.

The essay is the one thing that you have complete control over in the college application. You should feel empowered by this prospect. You can't go back and change that C grade you received in trig or in your freshman Spanish class. You can't go back and decide to play basketball all four years while also developing your talents as a bassoonist and leaving time for plenty of community service, and read the complete works of Shakespeare, purely for enjoyment. But you can decide how you're going to write your essay. In reality, you can go back and update an essay already written and, ironically, one that didn't get the grade you thought it should. You can't change the past, but you most definitely can write a piece in the present that will impact your future.

Many candidates I have met over the years express the view that the admissions essay is a kind of alien life form, something completely different from any species they have ever encountered. Do you think the college essay is like nothing you've ever done before? If you answered "yes," I respectfully disagree. Haven't you recently written an essay or paper for school? How did you do that?

First, you probably started by becoming familiar with the subject. You read the novel, or the chapters in the history textbook, or whatever. Then, you probably started exploring the issue more deeply, gathering various opinions through discussions in a group or with a friend. Maybe you did some initial library or online research. You may have gone back over your notes to see what the teacher had to say on the subject. Chances are you started by sketching some ideas out—maybe it was a formal outline, or maybe it was just some sentences representing the main points you wanted to make. As you continued, you probably connected the dots to create a rough draft. Later, you read through it, revised, shifted the order of a couple paragraphs, tweaked the wording to sound just right, and voila! You wrote your essay or paper.

Why should writing a college application essay be any different? It shouldn't! It should involve:

- Exploring the subject of the essay—you—and the question posed, if any
- Gathering opinions through discussions with others, through internal thoughts, and, ideally, through jotting down ideas on paper
- Conducting topic or school-specific research online or in the library
- Creating an outline or a collection of keywords and sentences, and then a rough draft
- Editing the draft until it is ready to be submitted
- Confidently repeating a process that you have done many, many times before, most likely with positive consequences—*BM*

Robert Massa

shares his philosophical and practical advice from a dual perspective:

As a college admissions officer for almost thirty years, I thought I had seen it all. Then, two years ago, I was suddenly thrust into the position of parent of a high school senior seeking admission to some of the nation's most selective colleges. You might say, "Wow, the kid of an admissions dean at a top university or college will have no problems. She'll do everything right because her dad will make sure of it!" Well, please be advised that while my daughter did have less angst than many of her classmates, it was more because she did the college search right than it was because her dad "took care of it." Therefore, as an admissions professional and as a parent, I have learned much about a process that should be anticipated with much enthusiasm and positive anticipation, not with anxiety.

College admissions is a multifaceted process. While this book focuses on essays, that hurdle is but one aspect of the journey. The major factor, as noted in Appendix 2 is to understand yourself—how you learn best, how you interact with others, and your general educational objectives—and then to match these characteristics with attributes of the colleges you are considering. In the admissions world, we call this "assessing the fit."

Obviously, when selecting target schools, you must also pay attention to factors such as the acceptance rate, the middle 50 percent of test scores, and the average GPA or rank-in-class. You will want to be solidly within the academic range in addition to possessing the personal characteristics that match the college's mission and vision. Whether an application requests it or not, you can write a supplemental essay explaining why you wish to attend this particular college or university—what you know about yourself and your goals and how this college will meet your needs better than any other institution.

College admissions officers love it when you play back to them the messages they try to convey in the college's brochure, particularly when you relate this to an understanding of yourself.

I have seen students write all sorts of wild and risky essays. My daughter wrote, as many students do, about the impact on her life of a parent—her mother. My wife battled breast cancer twice, once when my daughter was ten years old, and again when she was sixteen. The impact of the second diagnosis on my daughter was profound, and she was able to tell a story about her mother's battle that was both personal, yet focused on her mother.

A narrative that tells about a character other than yourself from your point of view does, in most cases, give the reader a clear sense of your values. In my daughter's case, it told the reader, without saying it literally, how her mother's trauma and her approach to dealing with it gave my daughter a new perspective on what was important in her life. She did this not in a factual or literal way, but through a narrative that told of a particular day and event in her mother's life and my daughter's participation in it. Without telling the reader about her anger and fear and her incredible respect for her mother's courage, my daughter was able to convey these things through her story. This is what makes the great essays stand out from the good ones. Never answer an essay question literally. Always tell a story that, through the narrative, conveys the message you want the reader to understand.

In Chapter 8, you will review one of the best essays I have read in my career. In this piece, you will see what I mean when I advise you to tell a story that answers a question in a nonliteral way. When you do read it, you should be able to create a list of bullets identifying its key elements and why it was effective. When you finish reading the chapters that follow, you should also be able to cite your own step-by-step approach to admissions essay writing. For now, I ask you to look back over all of the comments made by those with varied perspectives and begin to identify common elements.

Summarize what you, the reader, has learned so far, and what would be on your bullet point list. Admissions essay writing involves:

_____

_____

_____

_____

_____

_____

_____

_____

_____

So, each of us, including you, has now described our metaphorical elephant, the admissions essay writing process, from varying perspectives. As you reviewed each description, progressing page by page, and as you reflected on this entire chapter, you were able to formulate guidelines that parallel our previously cited six steps to essay writing success. While the phrases used by individuals might not be the same, and order of suggested steps might vary, concepts associated with the process of essay writing and the components of a good essay can be generalized and expressed in a common voice.

College admissions essay writing can and should include:

- Self-evaluation and an inventory of personal characteristics, attitudes, and achievements
- Identification of "good writing"—works completed by the applicant as well as those completed by others

- A positive attitude that focuses on diminishing anxieties and maximizing confidence
- Recognition that essay writing is already a part of your existing academic repertoire and a skill that can easily be applied to the specific task at hand
- Self-revelation, no matter the question, while focusing on topics and themes raised
- Confidence and creativity to not take questions literally
- Brainstorming topics and generating initial lists of keywords, simple sentences, or freeform paragraphs that will, later, be incorporated into a more structured draft
- Drafting using individualized styles, structured outlining, or component-by-component paragraph-building approaches
- Editing and proofreading processes that include grammatical, content, format, and stylistic reviews

As the essay writer, an individual who has a record of success, you must exhibit:

- Belief in your essay writing abilities
- Openness to seek the advice and editorial feedback of others
- Patience and persistence needed to do the best job possible

As you proceed, the content of each chapter will open your eyes a bit wider as more information is revealed. Soon, you will see sample essays and analyses, some before-and-after reviews, and a step-by-step essay critique. Knowledge of tips and techniques will inspire you to create admissions essays that others will be privileged to read.

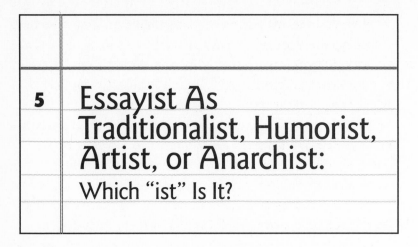

5 | Essayist As Traditionalist, Humorist, Artist, or Anarchist:
Which "ist" Is It?

LINGUISTS MIGHT SAY that "Been there, done that" is a phrase in the genre of California mall-speak, first used by teens in the 1980s. Today the phrase is commonly used, no matter the age or geographic locale of the speaker. For our purposes it has one specific meaning, which is this: It is crucial that you remember you have written essays before. Specifically, you have written great essays before! This chapter progresses from an academic exploration of general essay writing to practical strategies for tackling admissions essay themes and essay questions.

Essay writing is taught in elementary school and fine-tuned in secondary English classes. Skills are further developed in a variety of high school subject-specific classes, including science and history. As a result of training and achievements of the past, you are already an experienced essayist. Don't ever forget that! To reinforce this truth, and refresh your memory, let's reflect on the basics of traditional essay writing.

Traditionalists

Traditionalists write admissions essays with a clearly recognizable format. While different books (including those cited in Appendix 1) and various instructors may not agree on the number of steps involved in essay writing or on the phrases used to label each step, common elements are easy to identify. There are no impressionists or abstract word artists among those who paint pictures of essay writing techniques. With traditionalists, what you see is what you get. Or, what they say should be what you write.

As you undoubtedly already know, an essay has three components: a beginning, a middle, and an end. Your response to any question must be organized, logical, and well presented. Essays written for classes, including those that are written during the very nerve-wracking and stressful final exams, must reveal knowledge of certain topics and contain facts supporting particular hypotheses. Those written for college applications should, in all cases, be organized, thematic and, most important, self-revealing. As we first focus on general essays, not application essays, think about how traditional views apply to admissions essay purposes.

The introductory paragraph (occasionally more than one) tells readers what you are about to discuss, and it should offer glimpses into a series of word pictures that will yield a solid essay—ideally, one that captures the reader's attention. Avoid restating the essay question in the introduction. Rather, share interpretations of issues inspired by the question and present major themes you will address. The introduction, whether essays are course-specific or admissions focused, must allow readers to anticipate what will be covered. The first sentence of this paragraph is commonly called the "thesis sentence" because it introduces all that will follow within the succeeding sentences and paragraphs. A strong introduction will achieve at least two or more of the following:

- Reveal your interpretation of the question posed.
- Preview what the essay will cover.
- Overview any hypotheses, arguments, or key points to be made in subsequent paragraphs.

- Introduce or define keywords, key concepts, allusions, or metaphors presented in the essay question or in your approach to the essay answer.

Your body paragraphs (at least two, but often three or more, depending on word count and structure) support arguments or your hypothesis, contain text in line with "command words" or "question cues," and present both descriptive and analytical content. Clarity and order are required of those writing traditional essays for academic and admissions purposes. Those reading admissions essays also seek to learn something about the reader beyond facts, topical knowledge, and writing style.

Your concluding paragraph summarizes overall content, reinforces key points, and reveals any surprise images or "punch lines."

All essays, no matter how conservative, academic, or creative, should have recognizable structure and clear style. Structure and style may present a "which comes first, the chicken or the egg" conundrum. Some believe style results only from planning and implementation of predetermined essay structures. Others believe that thorough postdraft editing, addressing issues of structure, is how style is truly revealed. The truth is, it doesn't matter whether style follows structure or structure follows style. These complementary characteristics are required of all good pieces. Many traditionalists suggest the secret to structure and style is to treat each paragraph within your essay as a "mini-essay"; in other words, each paragraph should contain an introduction, a body, and a conclusion.

If you use the mini-essay approach, components of the paragraph are the introductory sentence, supporting sentences, and transition (or linking) sentence. The topic sentence summarizes or introduces what you are going to cover in the paragraph, or instills within readers the rough outline of an image that will be detailed later. Supporting sentences provide definition, evidence, analysis, or detailed images that flow from the topic sentence. Last, the transition sentence smoothly carries one paragraph to the next. Keep in mind that most well-crafted paragraphs contain at least three sentences and no more than six.

For many, a simple test of the quality of essay drafts involves writing only the introductory and transition sentences in order of their appearance. When you review just the first and last sentences of each paragraph, does the "bare bones" content seem logical and reveal all of the themes you wish to present? Would changing any of the introductory or transition sentences clarify the essay? Can you be a bit more creative with the transition sentences, setting up more "suspense and surprise" when the next introductory sentence is read?

"Plan your work and work your plan" is a phrase commonly used by coaches and teachers. This advice definitely applies to writing essays. Traditionalists and academicians advise essayists to begin planning by focusing on a topic. To do so you should identify, interpret, and then follow command words or question cues in the essay assignment. These words include, but are not limited to, the following:

- **Analyze:** Expand on causes and effects, examine motivations and reasons, and focus on "why" and "how"
- **Compare:** Focus on similarities and differences, magnifying similarities
- **Contrast:** Focus on similarities and differences, magnifying differences
- **Criticize:** Examine the merit of the essay, expanding upon strengths as well as weaknesses and focusing on your opinion
- **Define:** Clearly note topic parameters and all they encompass, and then focus on key components
- **Describe:** Offer facts, events, or actions, limiting interpretation and emphasizing the most important points

- **Discuss:** Cite and then support your opinion and those of others, magnifying facts that support both
- **Evaluate:** Present varied opinions on a subject, then focus on those you determine have the most merit

Some traditionalists overanalyze command words in order to determine "what they (those who assign and grade essays) want." It's not uncommon for traditionalists to look up definitions for every word preceding and following question cues. While this approach may seem compulsive, it can inspire actions and is a form of brainstorming. For many admissions essayists, it only delays the process. You can examine command words to plan and add structure to brainstorming, but do not dwell deeply on definitions. Remember, we are now reviewing traditional views on general essay writing, not focusing on admissions essay techniques.

After evaluating the essay question, writers are ready to jot down a few keywords of their own. Traditionalists do advise brainstorming, but most suggest using formal outlining techniques or structured listings of key concepts, followed by creation of "essay skeletons," "pyramids," or "blocks." Some involve formal outlining or simple fill-in-the-blank activities like this one:

Introductory Paragraph Topic Sentence / Essay Thesis Sentence:
Introductory Paragraph Supporting Sentence 1:
Introductory Paragraph Supporting Sentence 2:
Introductory Paragraph Supporting Sentence 3:
Introductory Paragraph Transition Sentence / Essay Thesis Sentence:
Body Paragraph 1 Topic Sentence:
Body Paragraph 1 Supporting Sentence 1:
Body Paragraph 1 Supporting Sentence 2:
Body Paragraph 1 Supporting Sentence 3:
Body Paragraph 1 Transition Sentence:
Body Paragraph 2 Topic Sentence:

Body Paragraph 2 Supporting Sentence 1:
Body Paragraph 2 Supporting Sentence 2:
Body Paragraph 2 Supporting Sentence 3:
Body Paragraph 2 Transition Sentence:
Concluding Paragraph 1 Topic Sentence:
Concluding Paragraph Supporting Sentence 1:
Concluding Paragraph Supporting Sentence 2:
Concluding Paragraph Supporting Sentence 3:
Concluding Paragraph and Essay Concluding Sentence:

The geometry of planning or prewriting steps isn't as critical as the fact that for traditionalists, structure is required of style and style arises from structure. Structure and clear style are evidenced for many authors and instructors by the "5 Ws and an H": "Who, what, where, when, why, and how?" All of these questions are addressed during essay planning, drafting, and editing. Traditional essayists answer the following questions:

- Who is your intended audience?
- What information is needed as determined by command words? What information is required by evaluation criteria?
- Where do you clearly present key points? Where do critical contents of the essay appear?
- When do you need to present factual information, opinions, or creative word images?
- Why are certain metaphors or images used?
- How are the metaphors or images creatively presented?

Some traditional essay writers create outlines after answering the previous questions. Others use outlining techniques, boxes connected with lines, or fill-in-the-blank sentence and paragraph grids. No matter what the approach, they follow a series of clearly defined and, frankly, rigid steps. Some who pass the traditionalist baton to those running the essay race identify prewriting, writing, revising, and proofreading as the components of good writing.

Prewriting for traditional essayists involves reading specific assignments, general periodicals, and works by inspirational authors; discussing the topic or related themes with friends, family, peers, or colleagues; engaging in personal reflection; brainstorming; list-making; graphic diagramming; identifying and narrowing down topics; determining your purpose statement; analyzing the target audience; creating a thesis or introductory sentence; and organizing all research materials and outlines.

Writing involves planning, creating, and then building paragraph upon paragraph. The five-paragraph essay is the most traditional approach and the one most often taught by advocates of traditional style. Before we continue our exploration of the traditional essay, let's look at some nontraditional approaches.

Humorist

Humorists write satirical pieces, comedic short stories, or scenes from a play or film.

Have you ever written something funny, on purpose? Really, was it funny? When others read this piece, including Mom and Dad, did they laugh out loud or did they simply offer a polite smirk? Humor is perhaps the most difficult approach to take when responding to admissions essay questions. If you have a history of humor, a record of generating giggles and guffaws, give it a try.

Have you successfully drafted, edited, and finalized short stories, scripts, or similar works? If you have never really attempted this style before, please wait until you've been admitted and you take a course in creative writing. For those few experienced humorists, some keywords of wisdom:

- Follow the rules of traditional essay writing as well as the A through F steps to success.

- Remember that humor can arise from planning as well as spontaneity.
- Before you write a humorous piece, identify and read at least two works you think are funny.
- Have others read the finished work and offer their views.
- If you submit scripts or pieces that vary far from the assignment, provide a brief cover page that explains why you did so and how developing this piece, and others like it, make you feel.

Artist

Artists create cartoons, videos, sketches, Web-based graphics and animated pieces, songs, and poems.

Those with a passion for artistic endeavors, and a history of creating pieces well received by others, can consider this option. Those who wish to be artistic for the first time are advised not to do so. While some schools offer this option explicitly, others may not understand your motivations. If you wish to broadly and boldly interpret stated questions and respond with an artistic submission, know why you are doing so and share these motivations in writing. If you do choose to put forth your artistic expressions:

- Create a new work that is inspired by your candidacy and reveals something pertinent to reviewers.
- Address software or other technical issues that might impact the ability of admissions professionals to review your piece.
- Before and while creating the work, think about themes, images, and topics that you must get across to the reader.
- Provide a supplemental page (a very brief essay or maybe just a paragraph) sharing with readers why you chose an artistic method to fulfill the criteria asked of you, how this piece reflects your attitudes as well as talents, and how

these talents might be used within the context of your college experience.

Anarchist

Anarchists write essays about why they hate writing essays, submit nothing at all, or replace or supplement essays with what they consider very creative expressions.

Some anarchists are humorists in disguise. They write about not liking to write with metaphorical tongues placed firmly in cheeks, revealing smirks of self-pleasure. Humor, especially sarcasm, is a challenging approach to take when writing admissions essays. Some can be creative and controversial without being confrontational. But using a risky strategy does not mean that your efforts will stand out in a positive way. If you have successfully written satirical pieces in the past, give it a try. If not, stick with traditional storytelling techniques to express "to write or not to write" dilemmas.

It is never a good idea to ignore instructions, or turn in your application without fulfilling the essay requirement. Even if you submit a piece written previously for a course assignment, with a brief supplemental note explaining why, you should offer something. Confrontational and oppositional actions or attitudes very rarely yield positive outcomes.

Some anarchists write essays and then supplement submissions with special items, manifesting what they believe to be "creative" pieces. We've heard stories about candidates writing essays on their target school's letterhead, and those who submit pictures of themselves wearing their target school's logo apparel. What about tales of candidates who submit applications accompanied by folding chairs, with an attached note stating "save a seat for me in the class of 2006"? Do applicants really send in shoes with a note stating "I can follow in the footsteps of those who succeeded at your school"?

Whether truths or myths, these tales do have lessons to teach. Tread paths littered with potholes very, very carefully, or take another route. You can proceed, knowing the risk of twisted ankles, as well as embarrassing falls on your backside, or avoid them. Clearly, if you are thinking about being creative, you have viable options, including the development of the most creative and expressive traditional essays possible. Allow essay writing to be the action that speaks loudly through well-written words.

The Traditionalist Might Be the Easy "ist"

As introduced earlier, the traditional essays have common elements and characteristics. This form of essay:

1. Is composed of an introductory paragraph, three body paragraphs, and a concluding paragraph
2. Begins with an introductory paragraph that uses a special "device" to attract the reader's attention, such as a philosophical question; a descriptive scene; an inspirational quotation; an unusual, surprising, or controversial opinion; a historical or current event; or a unique and brief story
3. Concludes the introductory paragraph with a thesis sentence that introduces readers to topics to be covered in body paragraphs as well as their order of presentation
4. Contains a body paragraph for each main topic; each starts with a topic sentence that is directly related to the thesis sentence in the introductory paragraph
5. Uses transitional sentences to connect each body paragraph
6. Follows a plan, revealing topics chronologically, in order of importance, or in ways to maximize surprise
7. Concludes with a paragraph that summarizes, emphasizes main ideas, reveals a surprise, or offers the final piece of any literary puzzles presented

Traditionalists all believe that structure is the prerequisite of good style. Many advocates of the traditional approach offer lists of "rules." One of the most popular reference books, *The Elements of Style* (see Appendix 1), offers lists that have been memorized by many writers over the years. These are a few of the book's key points:

- Choose a suitable design and hold to it.
- Make the paragraph the unit of composition.
- Use the active voice.
- Put statements in positive form.
- Use definite, specific, concrete language.
- Omit meaningless words.
- Avoid a succession of loose sentences.
- In summaries, keep to one tense.

These timeless tidbits are appropriate for all essay writers, including you, the admissions essayist. If you are a traditionalist, you will ultimately use "evaluation criteria" to determine whether the essay is finished. Subject-specific criteria include the presence of certain facts and, in many cases, content presented by instructors. More general evaluation criteria, utilized during the editing phase, are reflected by questions such as these:

- Did I respond directly or creatively to the essay question?
- Did details offered in each supporting body paragraph support the introductory paragraph and, specifically, the essay's topic sentence?
- Did I follow an obvious order, appear logical, and flow to a conclusion?
- Did I project a consistent and active voice, and follow grammar and structure guidelines?
- Did I use appropriate vocabulary, and is it clear, concise, and focused?
- Does my essay reveal my personality, values, interests, and hopes to readers?

- Did I reveal knowledge of the school or of special circumstances related to my candidacy?
- Can I omit sentences, use alternative words, or reorder sentence presentations?
- Is each sentence clear and necessary, serving the purposes of each paragraph and of the entire essay?

Traditional essay advice can, and often should be, applied to admissions essay writing. For some applicants, traditionalism offers ways to get started, via structured planning, and ways to finish, via focused editing and proofreading. College admissions essays are indeed specialized assignments, but they must follow all of the guidelines of good style and structure!

Some traditional English teachers, private college coaches, and school counselors characterize admissions essay writing as another six-step process. The steps and the goals associated with each are:

Prewriting and Planning: Focusing on the Topic
- The topic is "you," as well as that presented in the question.
- Focus on command words and question cues.
- Take inventory of cocurricular, athletic, and educational activities, and then evaluate which are most important and meaningful to you.
- Identify favorite classes and activities, citing the impact that these have had on your personal and intellectual growth.
- Clarify and articulate personal, academic, and career goals.
- Evaluate strengths as well as weaknesses, opportunities as well as challenges, and successes as well as failures.
- Cite most influential individuals, including family, teachers, friends, and those historical or famous individuals who inspire strong feelings.
- Note key concepts, themes, and words associated with the topic you have selected for your essay.

Prewriting and Planning: Identifying Details

- Note thoughts, behaviors, or realizations you want the essay to convey to the reader.
- Write a sentence that identifies what you want the essay to support (this is the essay's thesis sentence).
- List and prioritize details that will expand upon what you want to cover.
- Focus on visual, auditory, and emotional details.
- Determine the desired number of paragraphs.
- Create an outline or a list of topic sentences and transition sentences for each paragraph.
- Diagram, outline, or in some way structure the essay.
- List supporting details for topic sentences of each paragraph.

Writing: Drafting by Structure

- Fill in the outline by adding supporting sentences.
- At this point, don't be too concerned with grammar.
- When frustrated, review your outline or diagrams, examine lists of thoughts, talk to someone about the topic, or read inspirational writings.

Revising: Adding, Improving, and Deleting

- Review the draft paragraph by paragraph.
- Did you follow your plan, with each sentence and paragraph revealing a clear purpose?
- Did you respond to the topic?
- Do the introductory, supporting, and concluding paragraphs serve desired purposes, or should they be revised and reordered?
- Does the essay appear in a logical order and, ultimately, project a sense of unity?
- Does the essay reflect values, interests, and personality?
- Does the essay follow the predetermined structure?

Revising: Fine-Tuning
- Review this draft sentence by sentence.
- Do the topic sentences in each paragraph serve desired purposes, or should they be revised, reordered, or removed?
- Do the supporting and transition sentences in each paragraph serve desired purposes, or should they be revised, reordered, or removed?
- Do the thesis sentence and concluding sentence serve desired purposes, or should they be revised?
- Does the essay remain in proper tense and voice, focusing clearly on the target reader?
- Does the essay present the most important points among those outlined in prewriting and planning?

Proofreading
- Review this draft word for word.
- Does the essay follow rules of grammar and usage?
- Is it free of typos and spelling errors?
- Does it contain the correct references to school name, place, and institution-specific information?
- Do all of your supporting details show in the final draft?
- Do any revealing techniques maximize the sense of surprise, creativity, or humor?
- Are the vocabulary words that you chose to express all points and thoughts the most effective words you can use?
- Have another set of eyes, another brain, and another heart reviewed and commented on the essay?
- Listen to feedback, make final changes, and then "take ownership" of the final draft as yours.

Do these six steps seem vaguely familiar? They should! You can take a traditional approach, blending the above with our A through F steps to success: Assessment of personal characteristics and achievements, Brainstorming themes and topics, Choosing a topic or two, Drafting two essays, Editing both drafts, and Finalizing are compatible with the traditional approach.

It's as easy as ABC to author a great traditional admissions essay. You have already written some great essays, as assigned for various classes, and followed steps similar to those identified. But be aware that admissions essays are not exactly the same as academic essays. Comparing the differences between admissions essays and subject-specific or academic essays, you will become a better admissions essayist:

- Admissions essays do not focus on impressing the reader with specific facts.
- Admissions essays do not simply present information the reader wants to see.
- Admissions essays are not evaluated based upon the writer's understanding of concepts and facts.
- Admissions essays are not "graded" in an academic sense.
- Admissions essays focus on providing the reader information pertaining to the writer.
- Admissions essays reveal self-knowledge, rather than factual or conceptual knowledge.
- Admissions essays are evaluated based upon the writer's clarity of personal expressions and stated educational goals, and also upon matching these expressions and goals with admissions profiles and the school's educational offerings, priorities, and mission.
- Admissions essays are evaluated and, often, "scored," and they do impact a decision-making process.
- Admissions essays can be creative, and they veer from stated topics when appropriate.
- Admissions essays can be created via structured steps, yet be creative and effective.

Traditional admissions essayists follow the guidelines presented to create wonderful and effective pieces. Do not equate "traditional" with "typical" or "mediocre." Following traditional approaches and techniques can yield unique offerings that reveal things that others don't often see. Enhancing traditional steps with the suggestions in this handbook will ensure that this will be the case.

Now, let's examine styles of essayists who wander from the proverbial "beaten path." Those who stroll routes least taken are admired by poets, but do they gain the positive responses of admissions essay reviewers? In Chapter 6 you will learn about another "ist"—the strategist. These essayists, through planning and implementation, include school-specific references in their essays. For now, though, let's examine contributor opinions regarding which "ist" presented in this chapter is best. Each will share views on the power of traditional planning, writing, and editing techniques, and include a few anecdotes regarding how admissions professionals respond to the styles of humorists, artists, and anarchists.

Bridget

offering the perspective of college counselor, English teacher, and past admissions officer, comments:

I might be restating the obvious, but before drafting any essay, particularly admissions essays, establish your objective. Think about the following questions: Why am I writing this essay? What do I want to convey to the reader? How do I want the reader to perceive me? How will I approach writing this? What is my best writing style? Then, begin prewriting activities, including brainstorming ideas or essay themes; putting ideas on paper; considering your audience; and focusing on specific ideas and themes.

Next, outline your writing. You can use formal or informal outlining techniques, including creating a rough sketch of ideas.

Establish your tone and approach, whether humorous, intellectual, personal, quirky, informal, or formal. Make your tone clear and obvious and extend it throughout the essay. Develop initial ideas and themes in a first draft. After the first draft is completed, eliminate clutter and purge lofty, pretentious phrases, sentences, and ideas. Then rewrite, rewrite, and rewrite again, until the essay is yours and meets your highest standards. During the rewriting process you should share the draft with others, obtain feedback, and consider how the suggestions may or may not improve your work; save all pre-existing drafts before you write another (losing earlier versions is a common and anxiety-provoking mistake); read your draft out loud; and, last, make final corrections. Then take pride in your finished masterpiece!

A confident, "I can do it" attitude is very important because it encourages essayists to approach writing with a level of assertiveness and enthusiasm that will be well received by readers. Confidence in writing is essential at the beginning, in the middle, and at the end. There is no substitute for this kind of positive attitude.

Regarding "alternative approaches" taken by those you dramatically call "anarchists," I haven't found too many of the quirky approaches that work for me. If the admissions people wanted a poem, a whimsical poem, a drawing, etc., they would have asked for it. If they ask for an essay, they want an essay. If you're writing just for the sake of getting something down on paper, college admissions officials are going to see through your work. By all means, be creative, but stick to what is asked of you. Generally, there is plenty of room for creative freedom while still remaining within the parameters of the essay question.—*BK*

Jordan

who only a few years ago wrote admissions essays, and as a student still writes subject-specific essays regularly, adds:

Last semester I tutored in a middle school afterschool program. This meant digging into my past to remember fractions and percent calculations, revisiting earth science, and yes, of course, the return of the five-paragraph essay! As I helped my sixth-graders fill in their detailed outlines, with spaces for the topic sentence, then three interesting facts, followed by a concluding sentence, I realized that their writing style was not much different from my own. Sure, my professors were presenting me with very different topics to write about, but the fundamentals of writing remain the same for an essay about Sally Ride, a research paper about ethnic conflicts in the Middle East, or a personal essay destined for an admissions officer's desk. Once you realize that, the hard part is over. Now fill in the blanks, just as your fourth-grade teacher taught you long ago.

Of course your writing has improved over the years, with increased complexity and flow to your prose, but still that same formula applies. Start with some kind of outline. I will be the first to tell you that outlining is not my thing! I feel that it cramps my style, so I would much rather just write and worry about organization later. But, for a project that can already be a little intimidating, an outline is a way to take off the pressure. You must admit, even for those who get good grades on essays written for English or other classes, admissions essays are a bit intimidating. Once you've done outlining, prewriting, planning, or whatever you want to call it, your essay can grow strong and tall, even if you are answering that silly "If you were a tree, what kind would you be?" question.

I always find that if I am forced to outline I don't have enough room to say what I want in the few lines provided. So, after I outline I add a few lines here and a few lines there. Well there you go, suddenly your outline has become your rough draft. It really is that simple. There is no special language for college admissions writing. It's still English, it's still the same grammar, and it's still the same writing style you've been using all along.

Admissions essay readers are just a slightly different audience. And, yes, you must know your audience and your purposes for writing. Once you have written a great essay, you can add some reader- and school-specific twists in order to meet your goals.

I've heard those stories about students who did unusual things, rather than submit an essay, but, frankly, I've never met one. So, I don't know whether the stories are facts or myths. I guess I was and will always be more of a traditionalist, so the idea of trying to be funny or different never crossed my mind when I wrote my admissions essay. I just wanted to write a good essay. As I confessed earlier, for some of my schools, I revised and adapted an essay written for a competition. Again, good writing is good writing. At least that's what I believe. During college visits I heard many admissions counselors echo this thought, so as a trusting and traditional student, I believed them. I don't think great essays can get you into any particular school, but I did fear that a bad essay might negatively impact my chances of getting into one of my top choices. It took a lot of focus and many nervous writing and rewriting sessions, as well as the comments of others, to overcome my fear of negative consequences. But once I focused on the positive, and created the very best essays possible, everything seemed to flow. No matter how much pressure you feel, you can and will write a great essay! I did it. All of my friends and current classmates did it. And you will do it too!—*JN*

Robert

our wise and sage veteran of the admissions game, concludes:

I have probably read 15,000 college essays during my career in college admissions. That is a conservative estimate. The most successful essays from my perspective are those that tell a story and that give the reader a glimpse inside your soul. They follow the traditionalist approach outlined in this chapter, and they make the reader want to read on after the introduction because the introductory paragraph creates "suspense" or poses a question that is only partially answered.

On rare—and I do mean rare—occasions, humorous or artistic approaches do work. One particularly creative essay I remember helped a student to stand out because it used a combination of all three forms—traditional, humor, and art. As I recall, the essay attempted to give the reader a clear sense of the student's hobbies, interests, and commitments—sort of a "meaningful activities transcript" feel. Rather than writing a typical essay, this young man wrote a pictorial essay in which he and his friend "Stevie the Stress Ball" went through various events together. He showed pictures of "Stevie" (on whom he had painted a face and hair) at a baseball game, in front of the Statue of Liberty, on a roller coaster, reading to the elderly—you get the point. It was full of humor because it was written so seriously and illustrated with crazy photographs. But it was also structured and had a point. This young man was a serious student, but he relieved his stress by doing things he enjoyed doing, providing the reader with an understanding of this candidate's personality.

On the other hand, the attempted humor in the essay I read explaining how the writer drove his father's car into his neighbor's swimming pool flopped badly. Not only was it *not* funny, it showed mean irreverence that I found quite appalling. You can guess whether or not this candidate was accepted.

Most admissions essays submitted to selective colleges are good. Few are great, and there are always several that are pretty bad. It is better to write a good essay that does not set you apart in a competitive applicant pool than it is to take a risk that fails to help you get recognized by college admissions officials. The bottom line, though, is that only "great" or "terrible" essays serve to impact the admissions decision in a major way. In my experience, only 10 to

15 percent of the college essays I have read over the years fall into one of these categories. That doesn't mean that you shouldn't try to write a great piece. Get organized as suggested in this chapter, but also allow yourself to be creative in your essay by telling a story that reveals who you are. Again, the introductory paragraph should set the tone, but should also keep the reader guessing.

Finally, while it is certainly not necessary to do in your main essay, if the topic lends itself to it, weave in something specific about the college to which you are applying. For example, an applicant writing about an environmental service project in Honduras would be well advised to acknowledge a school's international studies and global education offerings and also the college's commitment to service. Do so if it fits nicely and logically into the essay. If not, it is always best to write a shorter, supplemental piece on how the college's strengths fit your interests and your strengths. Admissions officers do like to see applicants who are aware of themselves and how they might "fit" in to the college.—*RM*

You now realize how traditional essay writing lessons of the past can and should be applied to your admissions essay writing future. Your past successes will predict your future successes.

By now you also should be very eager to apply your well-tested talents and begin drafting admissions essays. Before you determine which "ist" you will be, let's examine the one we briefly mentioned earlier—the strategist—and the potential impact of the last bit of advice in Robert's comments. You're about to learn how strategists consciously and confidently utilize their heads, in addition to their hearts.

6 | Strategic Thinking
Meets Emotional Expression

EVER WONDER ABOUT that big circle with the little circles and squiggly line on the tie-dyed T-shirts your mom and dad wore when they were teens? While the yin-yang symbol was popular in the 1960s, the symbol has been around for thousands of years, illustrating the ancient Chinese understanding of natural relationships. The outer circle represents "everything," while the black and white shapes within the circle represent the interaction of two energies, "yin" (black) and "yang" (white). Neither section of the circle is completely black or white, just as things in life are not completely black or white, and they cannot exist without each other. While "yin" would be dark, passive, downward, cold, contracting, introverted, and weak, "yang" would be bright, active, upward, hot, expanding, extroverted, and strong. The symbol represents interdependence of yin to yang and yang to yin, and the relationships of contrasting forces in nature.

The yin of essay writing is symbolized by "the head of the essayists," representing all that is preplanned, analyzed, and completed with targeted goals in mind. The yang of this process is "the heart of the essayists," encompassing all that is associated with feelings, self-reflections, revelations, beliefs, and hopes. To complete all proactive and reactive steps of admissions essay writing, both are required. While you might be emotional rather than rational, more like Dr. McCoy than Mr. Spock, you must become aware of the need for complementary motivations, strategies, and outcomes. When writing admissions essays you are a superior leader balancing intellect and emotion, yet boldly going where many have gone before.

The heart of the essayist wishes to first draft in freeform; then look within and write; loosely and independently edit; and, last, quickly send essays to schools, allowing fate to take its course. The heart allows for revelation of personal beliefs and values. It motivates writers to share meaningful narratives and express personal views as allusions and metaphors. This heartfelt perspective is, of course, natural, courageous, creative, and crucial. A great admissions essay must, as the title of an earlier exercise reflects, reveal to readers "the me that others don't often see." Your essay will do just that.

Self-assessment brings to the surface heartfelt expressions that otherwise might not appear in essay drafts or final versions, and it facilitates selection of particular questions. Reflection on emotional and personal issues does, as the process continues, lead to analysis and decision-making. Assessment and brainstorming, the first two of the six steps to essay writing, are very much influenced by intuition and emotion, both heart-driven factors. Choosing one or two topics, and, subsequently, drafting two essays are steps that require a balance of both heart and head. Editing and finalizing are completed best if the head is involved and structure is incorporated into style.

The head of the essayists always thinks about logic, structure, and format, consciously outlining, planning, and building the essay piece by piece. The head of the essayist conducts detailed editing and proofreading, seeks the advice and feedback of significant others, and, often, incorporates well-conceived school-specific references into each essay. This perspective is analytical, comprehensive, and crucial.

A great admissions essay must reflect structure as well as style. Your essay will be a literary reflection of both head and heart.

When completing assessment activities you became familiar with thoughts and feelings of self, with those of others who know you, and with information pertaining to particular colleges and universities. The Institution Inspiration and Image Inventory examined how much you knew about schools that are of interest to you. Look back at your answers to this particular exercise. Soon, you will know when and how to blend knowledge of schools you are applying to with the knowledge of yourself. You will learn how, if you wish, to make strategic references to campus visits, to Web-based research, or to conversations with students and alumni.

When you create your admissions essay, you will look back and project ahead. You will apply feelings as well as logic. You will enhance creativity through structured analysis. You will do all of this by merging traditional essay writing perspectives and techniques with the approaches of the strategist.

In Chapter 5 you learned that traditionalists, using "head of the essayist" approaches, find little difficulty getting started because they undertake structured planning and they work diligently toward completion of predetermined goals, using focused editing and proofreading techniques. In most cases, they plan and subsequently create essays that contain five or more paragraphs. These essays contain an introductory paragraph that overviews all that will be covered in the essay and begins with the crucial head-thought thesis statement; body paragraphs that reveal descriptive and analytical content supporting the thesis statement; and a concluding paragraph that summarizes overall content, reinforces key points, and reveals any surprises.

Traditionalists treat each paragraph as a mini-essay and edit until the topic sentence, supporting sentences, and transition sentences within each are clear, structured, and concise. With heads full of rules, editing questions, and structured diagramming, these essay-ists find and correct errors of format as well as content. By using these traditional approaches, they also determine if enough self-revelation and emotional expression is contained within essay drafts.

Strategists go beyond these techniques to identify ways to reveal that they have researched schools they are applying to, and that they have identified issues of personal import. They incorporate key issues, through a few sentences or a paragraph, into essays or into supplemental statements. Strategic issues most often have to do with these aspects:

- Size of institution
- Location
- Mission, educational philosophy, or strategic plan
- Curriculum; specifically, required "core and majors courses" and prerequisites
- Nature of particular academic offerings, including majors, minors, or clusters
- Overseas studies or special co-op, internship, or off-campus programs
- Particular faculty, and their research or field-specific interests
- Recent academic, cocurricular, or residential changes or community-related current events
- Student's familial history associated with the institution
- Student's curiosity pertaining to the research and academic interests of specific departments

While strategists do, when planning or editing, decide to address these issues in essays or supporting materials, they never do so insincerely. Those reviewing your writings will perceive insincerity as quickly as they will strategy. In this undertaking, your heart is as important as your head. You must truly care about the issues you raise, not just share "see what I know" content.

To identify and use strategic sentences or paragraphs, first review printed admissions literature and Web-based offerings. Using the head of the essayist, analyze these resources as if you are critiquing or evaluating copy, content, and format. When determining whether to include strategic references, answer the following for each school:

What are some identifiable "thesis sentences" of printed and Web resources, as they are revealed page by page or section by section?

_____

_____

_____

_____

_____

Which three to five supporting and concluding paragraphs in printed literature or on Web sites are the most interesting?

_____

_____

_____

_____

What are three to five specific themes clearly cited in printed or Web-based resources?

_____

_____

_____

_____

_____

_____

Once identified, which two or three statements, themes, or images do you find personally most appealing?

_____

_____

_____

_____

_____

What particular statements, if any, in these resources are naturally associated with essay topics you will be addressing?

_____

_____

_____

_____

_____

If answers to the first four queries generate a great deal of information, yet your response to the last is "none," do not try to push the metaphorical round peg into the square hole. Do not force school-specific references into your essay if they are not a good fit. You can incorporate the data you've gathered into supplemental statements, rather than essays, and the information will most definitely help you to make decisions regarding which admissions offer to accept.

If you have not already done so, review your answers to The Institution Inspiration and Image Inventory presented earlier. Responses should identify issues of personal interest as well as school-specific topics. Again, assessment is done with the heart, and editing with the head. As you determine whether to add some strategic school references, reviewing your assessment exercises can only be helpful.

In most cases, references to statements, themes, and images appearing in admissions literature are presented in concluding essay paragraphs. These references should be in the same literary style and voice throughout the entire piece. References to building names, mottos, school colors, mascots, or campus points of interest are subtle ways to reveal strategic knowledge while maintaining the existing literary integrity of the essay.

Web searches also can allow you to find and review speeches recently made by deans and presidents of your target schools, which should give you additional insights regarding the institution. Quotes from these speeches are not so subtle, but they do reveal your research skills. Using school-specific lexicons (and every school has special names for persons, places, and things) is another way to let readers know that you care enough to learn their language. You can learn school-specific phrases by speaking with currently enrolled students or alumni, and by reviewing student newspapers, magazines, and literary publications.

Please do not allow strategic desires to transform a balanced and well-structured narrative and stylistic piece into a blatant "I'm your candidate, because I know about your school" essay. Determine whether to add a few metaphorical pinches of salt or special garnish to your finished creation, but don't overcook or heavily season the literary meal you've created. You might want to offer a taste to someone whose opinion you trust. Ask a counselor, teacher, friend, or parent to read your final draft and tell you honestly whether adding some school-specific references would enhance or diminish the essay's impact.

Keep in mind that no matter how creative the essay, thoughts must balance feelings when you edit. Even if during the editing of your essay you determine that school-specific references are best made in supplemental statements, you should complete the following "True or False" quiz. As you progress down this list of questions, you will see that all answers must be affirmative. If they are not, you need to continue fine-tuning your essay until you reach the proper proportions of head and heart.

True or False?

1. The thesis statement of or initial image presented in my essay is clear and meaningful.
2. Each sentence of my essay flows logically from the one preceding, and transitions smoothly to the next.
3. Each paragraph of my essay flows logically from the one preceding and transitions smoothly to the next.
4. Each sentence of my essay is well conceived and has a purpose.
5. Each paragraph of my essay contains clear topic, supporting, and transition sentences.
6. The introductory paragraph offers an overview or image critical to the entire essay.
7. The closing paragraph of my essay provides closure, surprise, and/or insight into who I am as an individual.
8. The voice used throughout my essay is consistent and clearly identifiable.
9. When I use pronouns, they clearly refer to who or what I'm writing about.
10. My essay is written in an active voice.
11. My essay has a clear beginning, middle, and end, presenting an entire story.
12. My essay is not too long, nor too short, meeting quantitative and qualitative standards.
13. My essay delivers a message that is clear to readers.
14. Others have read drafts of my essay, noting errors, and offering comments as well as suggestions.
15. I have revealed at least two things about myself in my essay.
16. I am proud of the final essay.
17. I have consciously chosen whether or not to add school-specific references in my essay.
18. I have consciously chosen whether or not to add a supplemental statement with school-specific references.

Did you ace this quiz? If all answers were "yes," you did. If not, think about the "no" answers, review and edit your essay, and take it again. Remember, your admissions essay will reflect writing talents while revealing both your thoughts and feelings.

As you proceed, the content of each chapter will enhance emotional and intellectual perspectives as more information is revealed. Soon, you will see typical topics, sample essays and analyses, some before-and-after reviews, and a step-by-step essay critique. Knowledge of tips and techniques will inspire you to create admissions essays that others will be privileged to read. Use of these approaches to effectively unify and reveal strategic thoughts and emotional views in your essays.

7	# Typical Topics
	## Inspiring Exemplary Essays

MY GRANDFATHER WOULD always say, "It's six of one and a half-dozen of the other." While it took me a while to decipher his often-cited word puzzle, I now echo its lesson to others. No matter how many ways one looks at something and analyzes it, you reach only one conclusion. In the same vein, while you might be able to identify many, many different long and short admissions essay questions, very few themes appear over and over. No matter how much you analyze, fret, or fear, the truth is that there are fewer than two dozen topics and themes that encompass all college admissions essays. Most essay questions ask writers to address issues related to:

- Accomplishments and pride
- Activities and interests
- Art, drama, and music
- Autobiographical self-portraits
- Careers and ambitions
- College academics and college life
- Current events and world issues
- Dilemmas, ethics, and morals
- Disappointments and failures

- Diversity
- Family and friends
- Influential real, historical, or fictional persons
- Life experiences
- Quotations
- Travel or life overseas
- Risks
- Science, technology, and discoveries
- Sports
- Values and philosophies

Just in case you don't believe that there is a finite number of themes shared by authors historical and hysterical, from William Shakespeare to Stephen King, look again at those presented in the previous list. They do seem vaguely familiar, don't they? You've discussed them in classes and, perhaps, shared your ideas about them on paper before. Soon, you will do it all over again, and write about these topics on your college admissions applications.

The following are questions for essays that were recently required as part of the applications of a number of well-known schools. As you will see, familiar and recognizable themes are revealed within the questions of quite a few institutions. In reality, the common application (often called "common app") questions are shared by many schools. The common app is easily accessible online, and many schools accept it. Essay questions for the common app do vary from year to year, and school-specific instructions must be followed. Questions for a recent year included these:

- Evaluate a significant experience, risk you have taken, or ethical dilemma you have faced, and its impact on you.
- Discuss some issue of personal, local, national, or international concern and its importance to you.

- Indicate a person who has had a significant influence on you and describe that influence.
- Describe a character in fiction, a historical figure, or a creative work (as in art, music, science, etc.) that has had an influence on you, and explain that influence.
- Write on a topic of your choice.

Here are seventy-three questions you might expect to find on an application specific to a school you are applying to. Some of the questions are preceded by statements from the school's application.

- What idea, invention, discovery, or creation do you think has had the biggest impact on your life so far? Briefly explain.
- If you were given one year to spend on behalf of others, what would you choose to do, and why?
- What particular accomplishment up to this point in your life has given you the greatest satisfaction? Briefly explain.
- Describe a particular interest or activity that has been meaningful to you.
- There are limitations to what grades, scores, and recommendations can tell us about any applicant. We ask you to write a personal essay that will help us to get to know you better. In the past, candidates have written about their families, intellectual and extracurricular interests, ethnicity or culture, school and community events to which they have had strong reactions, people who have influenced them, significant experiences, personal aspirations, or topics that spring entirely from their imaginations. You should feel confident in writing about what matters to you, since you are bound to convey a strong sense of who you are.
- In what ways is a scientific or research-focused environment a good choice for you? In answering this question, discuss the role scientific curiosity plays in your life. In addition to this essay, you may (but are not required to) submit any research

paper or report on a science or engineering project you have written.

In addition to your interest in studying science and/or engineering, we are interested in knowing about you as a person. To this end, write an essay on one of the following:

- What event or events have shaped your life?
- Select one activity outside math and science in which you have been involved, and describe why it has been meaningful to you.
- Please fill the rectangle you see below with something interesting. Be creative!

(As the author, I wish to interject and note that contrary to a commonly used phrase, this last question is an example of a creative "thinking inside the box" option. Candidates should be sensitive to the fact that they are applying to a "techie think tank" type of school when completing this task. Also, an explanation of what you drew or copied and pasted would be an appropriate supplemental statement. For assignments like this one, focus on the nature of the school you are applying to, and do accompany your efforts with a supplemental page.)

- Life brings many disappointments as well as satisfactions. Could you tell us about a time when you experienced disappointment or faced difficult or trying circumstances? How did you react?
- We want to get to know you as a person. Make up a question that is personally relevant to you, state it clearly, and answer it. Feel free to use your imagination, recognizing that those who read it will not mind being entertained.
- We know you lead a busy life, full of activities, many of which are required of you. Tell us about an activity you pursued for the pleasure of it.

- Although you may not yet know what you want to major in, which department appeals to you, and why?
- What personal characteristics do you most value in yourself?
- What characteristics do others most value in you?
- Of the activities, interests, and experiences listed previously, which is the most meaningful to you, and why?
- Sharing intellectual interests is an important aspect of university life. Describe an experience or idea that you find intellectually exciting, and explain why.
- Relate a personal experience that reveals something about you to your future college roommate.
- Attach a small photo of something important to you and explain its significance.
- Risk comes in many forms, exploring an idea, bridging a social divide, confronting one's fears. Reflect on a risk you have taken and introduce us to your thoughts.
- Describe the courses of study and the unique characteristics of our university that most interest you. Why do these make you a good match for our university?

Please also respond to one of the following:

- You have just completed your 300-page autobiography. Please submit page 217.
- First experiences can be defining. Cite a first experience that you have had and cite its impact on you.
- Recall an occasion where you took a risk that you now know was the right thing to do.

Please answer the following questions. Please limit your answers to no more than one or two paragraphs. We recognize that all good writers seek feedback, advice, or editing before sending off an essay. When you have completed your essay, please tell us whose advice you sought for help, the advice he/she provided, and whether you incorporated his/her suggestions.

• If you are applying to our School of Arts and Sciences, please discuss why you consider our university and this particular school a good match for you. Is there something in particular at our university that attracts you?

• If you are applying to our School of Engineering, please discuss why you want to study engineering.

Please answer one of the following questions. We ask that you limit your essay to no more than two or three pages and use double spacing if the essay is typed or computer printed. Remember, this is your opportunity to speak to us in your own voice, so be yourself.

• Have you witnessed a person who is close to you doing something that you considered seriously wrong? Describe the circumstances, your thoughts, and how you chose to respond. If you discussed it with the person, was his/her justification valid? In retrospect, what, if anything, would you have done differently, and why?

• What has been your most profound or surprising intellectual experience?

• Write on any topic of importance to you. If you have written a personal essay for another purpose—even an essay for another college—that you believe represents you, your writing, and your thinking particularly well, feel free to submit it.

Applicants are asked to respond to one of the five questions in a page or two.

• Storytelling is an integral part of the formation of our identities. The stories that our parents and our communities tell us about themselves and the world form our first map of the universe. At some point, we begin to tell our own stories to ourselves and to others. Tell us a story you tell. Your story does not have to be either true or a story you would think to tell anyone but yourself; but the story must be your own, and its telling should have significance to you. Your story should also be significant to a listener who might tell a story about you.

- How do you feel about Wednesday?

- The Sudanese author Tayeb Salih wrote, "Turning to left and right, I found I was halfway between north and south. I was unable to continue, unable to return." If he is unable to choose, the character faces the threat of being frozen in place or torn between two states. Describe a halfway point in your life—a moment between your own kind of "north" and "south." Tell us about your choice, your inability to choose, or perhaps your folly in thinking there was ever a choice to be made.

- In his book *Through the Looking Glass*, Lewis Carroll imagines a fantastic, nonsensical world for Alice after she walks through a misty mirror. Physicist Stephen Hawking has speculated that a black hole, not a looking glass, might someday take us to many parallel universes. Three years ago, *The Matrix* mixed a bit of science with Carroll's fiction to create Thomas Anderson, a contemporary Alice who discovers that the "real" world is in fact a computer-generated dream. Explore the idea of a parallel world through the eyes of a philosopher, an artist, a theologian, a psychologist, or a scientist, or from any perspective you choose. How would you find this alternate reality? Who or what would take you there (by choice or by accident)? Would you or could you be a different person in each world?

- In the spirit of adventurous inquiry, pose an untraditional or uncommon question of your own. The answer to your question should display your best qualities as a writer, thinker, visionary, social critic, sage, sensible woman or man, citizen of the world, or future citizen of our university. Remember, this is about "adventurous inquiry." Be sure that you actually use a question of your own.

Below is a list of the essay questions—we call them "personal statements"—that appear in the 2003–04 application for admissions. Students are asked to choose one of the four topics and respond in a 400- to 500-word essay.

- Who is the voice of your generation and what message does he/she express? Do you agree with this message, and why?
- One theory holds that great leaders are produced by the particulars of their time. In your opinion, are great leaders the product of circumstance or the result of their individual qualities? Pick a leader and support your position.
- There is a significant difference between a stupid mistake and a clever one. Give an example of a "clever" mistake you have made and explain how it benefited you or others.
- When asked by Pope Boniface VIII to prove his skill as an artist, Giotto (1276–1337) drew a perfect circle freehand. What seemingly simple action would demonstrate your ability or skill, and how would it represent you?
- Create an acronym that represents your life. What is it, and what does it stand for?
- Imagine you are the offspring of any two famous people. Who are your parents, and what qualities have they passed on to you?
- Driving into downtown Chicago, there is a building visible from the Kennedy Expressway adorned with a mural of well-known Chicago personalities. If you could paint anything (other than your own likeness) on the building, what would it be, and why?

In the spirit of our university's tradition of collaborative learning, please provide us with an original essay topic or short statement you'd like to see on next year's application. (Most of this year's essays and short statements were suggested by students.)

• The quality of our university's academic life and the residential college system is highly influenced by the unique life experiences and cultural traditions each student brings. What perspective do you feel you will be able to share with others as a result of your own life experiences and background? Cite a personal experience to illustrate this. Most applicants are able to respond in two to three double-spaced pages.

• Please respond to the following using whatever space and medium you like. If you had only $10 to plan a day's adventure, where would you go, what would you do, and whom would you take with you?

• Write an essay on a topic of choice. Your essay should allow us to develop a sense of your effectiveness in written communications, and to understand more fully who you are and what you value.

• Discuss the factors that have led you to consider our university.

• All applicants: The Admissions Committee would like to know more about you in your own words. Please submit a brief essay, either autobiographical or creative, which you feel best describes you. If transferring from a four-year institution, please include your reasons for transferring from your present institution.

• Applicants to our College of Arts and Science: Please relate your interest in studying at our university to your future goals. How do these thoughts relate to your chosen course of study?

The following two essays are critical in the admissions selection process at our university. Use them to give the Admissions

Committee insight into your character and intellect. They should be written in multiparagraph form on additional attached sheets with your name and address. Answer both questions 1 and 2.

- What is your academic passion?
- What do you expect from your four years in college? How do you hope to change?

Short Essay: Choose one (please limit your answer to 250 words or no longer than half a single-spaced page):

- A legendary professor has often said that our faculty learn as much from their students as their students learn from them. Assume, for a moment, that you follow in this faculty member's footsteps and find yourself teaching a group of our university students. What would you hope to learn from them?
- The best writing is often very personal. All kinds of experiences—serious, funny, unexplained, fleeting—can influence our lives and help make us who we are. Tell us about a person, place, or event in your life that has particular meaning for you and why it is important to you. We'd especially like to hear about something that has affected your life that may not have been noticed by other people.
- Describe the future.
- Pick a value or an ideal that is important to you and describe a situation where you behaved in a manner that was inconsistent with that value.
- Select a creative work—a novel, film, poem, musical piece, painting, or other work of art—that has influenced the way you view the world and the way you view yourself. Discuss the work and its effect on you.

- Evaluate a significant experience, achievement, risk you have taken, or ethical dilemma you have faced and its impact on you.
- Discuss some issue of personal, local, national, or international concern and its importance to you.
- Indicate a person who has had a significant influence on you, and describe that influence.
- Describe a character in fiction, a historical figure, or a creative work (as in art, music, science, etc.) that has influenced you, and explain that influence.

It is up to you to decide what you want to tell the admissions committee. In the past years, many topics have been addressed, including the following:

- Interest/experience in your chosen major.
- State or national recognition for talent, creative ability, leadership, or academic achievement.
- An ethnic or cultural background or an age group that would add diversity to our campus.
- Extenuating circumstances that have significantly affected an otherwise strong academic record.
- Evaluate a significant experience, achievement, accomplishment, risk you have taken, or ethical dilemma you have faced, and its impact on you.
- At our university, our campus community comprises a diverse student body. Describe an aspect of your personality, experiences you have had, or things you have learned that will help you contribute to our diversity.
- Describe a living person, a character in fiction, historical figure, or a creative work (art, music, science, etc.) that has had an influence on you and explain that influence.
- If you could have invented anything from history, what would you pick, and why?

- If you could wake up tomorrow and learn that the major newspaper headlines were about you, what would you want them to say, and why?

Complete one of these essays:

- What is the best advice you have ever received? And did you follow it?
- Evaluate a significant event or achievement that has special meaning to you.
- Discuss some issue of personal, local, national, or international concern and importance to you.

Choose two of the following:

- Tell us about yourself. We know which activities you do and what your academic record looks like, but what don't we know? What fun, cool, or interesting things about you won't fit on the application? Feel welcome to be clever or funny, or write in a way that reflects your personality.
- What troubles you most about the world around you?
- Assuming the obligation and opportunity to change your world, where would you start and how would you use technology in your endeavor? Describe your cause, why it's worthwhile, and your proposal for its resolution.

Remember, topics that schools select are not related to the prestige of the institution or selectivity of the admissions process. Questions of all schools will be similar and will share common themes, if they're not from the common app. As you read the following list, do not try to match which institution posed each question, but do be enthused by the familiarity you now have with the content and intent of essay queries.

The schools that utilized these questions are Brandeis University, Bryn Mawr College, California Institute of Technology, Carnegie Mellon University, Dartmouth College, Dickinson College, Duke University, Emory University, Georgetown University, Harvard University, Harvey Mudd College, Johns Hopkins University, Massachusetts Institute of Technology, New York University, Northwestern University, Princeton University, Rice University, Stanford University, University of Chicago, University of Illinois at Urbana-Champaign, University of North Carolina at Chapel Hill, University of Pennsylvania, University of Rochester, Vanderbilt University, Wake Forest University, Washington University in St. Louis, and Yale University. Questions were available via the Internet; you can always access the most up-to-date topics and approaches with just a point and click to the "dot-edu" of your choice.

The contributors agree that there are no "right or wrong" answers to admissions essay questions, so inspiration and enthusiasm are the key factors that will influence which question you choose to answer and how quickly you begin writing. Let's diminish anxiety and enhance excitement with a bit of brainstorming.

Of course, you can see that we are continuing down the alphabetical path toward completion of the six steps to essay writing success. Now that you are familiar with common themes and actual questions, you are ready for the second step. But, please, do review answers to self-assessment inventories before you proceed. As you recall, some of the inventory questions previewed actual admissions essay queries. Your fill-in-the-blank answers should enhance the brainstorming that follows.

To begin brainstorming, please read the bullet comments following each of these themes, which you will remember from the beginning of this chapter. Note your immediate and brief responses to the questions posed.

Accomplishments and Pride

- Tales of significant personal, academic, extracurricular, or athletic events offering insight into your motives and lessons learned, not simply "stories about events"
- Glimpses into how you thought and felt before and after particular events or achievements and how "pride" may have inspired you to take on new activities or behaviors
- Vivid discussions, not just descriptions, about your feelings before, during, and after these events and how these new feelings might impact your future as a college student, and beyond

What accomplishments will reveal the most to someone who has never met you?

_____

_____

_____

_____

_____

_____

_____

_____

_____

Activities and Interests

- Revelations regarding why you do what you do, not just descriptions of what you do and for how long
- Emotional, intellectual, and personal growth that has resulted from cocurricular activities and avocations
- Lessons learned from activities conducted beyond the classroom
- Exploration of why you do the things you do, when you are truly free to make choices

What activities and interests will reveal things about you that most people don't know or suspect?

_____

_____

_____

_____

_____

Art, Drama, and Music

- Reactions to or impact of art, dramatic productions, or music created by others
- Revelations about art, dramatic productions, or music created by you
- Examinations of what you felt or thought about, not simply the circumstances regarding the production or piece of art
- Insights regarding your motives, enhanced skills, and changed perspectives related to artistic, dramatic, or musical endeavors

What artistic, dramatic, or musical programs that you attended would be most intriguing for others to learn about?

_____

_____

_____

_____

What pieces of art have impacted you the most, and what emotions and thoughts did they inspire?

_____

_____

_____

_____

What personal artistic, dramatic, or musical creations of yours can reveal motivations and feelings to others?

_____

_____

_____

_____

_____

Autobiographical Self-Portraits

- Reflections, noting how others perceived you or how you perceived yourself in the past
- Projections, noting how you wish others to perceive you or how you wish to perceive yourself in the future
- Emotional and physical word portraits revealing internal thoughts and feelings as well as external descriptions and personal reactions to physical characteristics
- Creative approaches like headlines, obituaries, birth announcements, and specific pages of biographies

What are the hidden qualities you want others to know about?

_____

_____

_____

_____

What are the obvious visual characteristics that inspire feelings in you that you can share with others?

_____

_____

_____

_____

_____

What key life anecdotes reveal the most about you, your relationships, and the way you view yourself and others?

_____

_____

_____

_____

_____

Careers and Ambitions

- Focused goals as well as fantasies or sparks of curiosity regarding particular careers
- Dreams about careers, college achievements, athletics, and extracurricular activities
- Real or fictional role models who personify your ambitions and sense of self
- Careers you would like to explore or that you have explored actively or cognitively

What career goals or curiosities have you shared with others, and what are those you have never shared?

_____

_____

_____

_____

What emotions and questions are inspired by thoughts of role models, real or fictional—individuals you have met or those presented in television, books, or films?

_____

_____

_____

What if circumstances forced you to change career goals; where would your interests focus?

_____

_____

_____

_____

_____

College Academics and College Life

- Anecdotes shared by family, friends, and tour guides
- Hopes and fears about future academic, athletic, or extra-curricular activities
- Anxieties and aspirations regarding residential life, relationships, and how others will treat you
- Dreams versus realities of college

What expectations, positive or not, have you not shared with others?

_____

_____

_____

_____

_____

_____

What do you anticipate your first semester and last semester will be like academically and emotionally?

_____

_____

_____

_____

_____

Which of your views about college are based on fact and which views are based on hearsay?

_____

_____

_____

_____

_____

In what ways do you learn best, and what motivates you to learn?

_____

_____

_____

_____

_____

Current Events and World Issues

- Educated opinions as well as emotional reactions
- Intellectual analyses as well as personal reactions
- Current events inspiring future curiosities and questions to investigate
- Personal or family circumstances impacted by current events or world issues, past or present
- Anecdotes regarding observations or interactions with those impacted by current events or world issues

What recent or current newspaper headlines or television news stories most intrigue you?

_____

_____

_____

_____

_____

What recent or current news stories relate to your academic interests?

_____

_____

_____

_____

_____

_____

_____

_____

What current events or world issues have had the most direct or indirect impact on you or your families?

_____

_____

_____

_____

_____

_____

_____

What events or issues inspired feelings and opinions that you have not yet shared with others?

_____

_____

_____

_____

_____

_____

_____

_____

Dilemmas, Ethics, and Morals

- Personal stands on controversial issues
- Actual circumstances generating moral dilemmas or concerns
- Thoughts about moral or ethical dilemmas appearing in books, plays, movies, or television productions
- Curiosity or concerns about moral issues presented by and stands taken by others.
- Defining "right and wrong" in as few words as possible
- Issues you have changed your views on over time

What are issues that might generate the most controversy in typical conversations with friends and family?

_____

_____

_____

_____

_____

What personal moral stand would most surprise friends and family?

_____

_____

_____

_____

_____

What circumstances that you have been involved in have truly addressed moral or ethical issues?

_____

_____

_____

_____

_____

What circumstances that family or friends have been involved in have truly addressed moral or ethical issues?

_____

_____

_____

_____

_____

_____

Disappointments and Failures

- Academic, athletic, cocurricular, or personal disappointments or failures
- Hidden failures or disappointments that no one else knows about, and public failures
- Reactions of others to your failures and disappointments
- Lessons learned from failures or disappointments experienced yourself or observed in others
- "If I had it to do over again" reactions to disappointments and failures
- Failures transformed into achievements

Which disappointments or failures would most surprise family and friends if they learned how you felt?

_____

_____

_____

_____

_____

_____

_____

_____

What do you consider your greatest disappointments within academic, athletic, cocurricular, or personal areas?

_____

_____

_____

_____

_____

What failures or disappointments of family or friends have truly had an impact on you?

_____

_____

_____

_____

_____

Diversity

- Ethnic and racial diversity in academic, workplace, or other settings
- Cultural and religious diversity at home or abroad
- Diversity issues or questions that make you the most frustrated or torn
- Anecdotes observed or read about that illustrate issues related to diversity
- Most and least diverse circumstances you have experienced

Which diversity issues inspire passion or frustration?

_____

_____

_____

_____

_____

What stories about diversity do family and friends tell, and what would you like to say to those who share these stories?

_____

_____

_____

_____

_____

_____

What fears do you have regarding issues related to diversity in college and university settings?

_____

_____

_____

_____

_____

Family and Friends

- How they perceive or would describe you
- What they truly do not know about you that would surprise them the most
- Lessons learned vicariously by observation or interactions with them
- Characteristics you most admire in others
- Those individuals who have most impacted your thoughts, feelings, and actions to date
- Those individuals who have spent the most chronological time with you
- Those individuals who have spent the most intellectual time with you
- Those individuals who have spent the most emotional time with you

What would you have liked the individuals in the four cate-gories listed previously to know about you, but you were afraid to tell?

_____

_____

_____

_____

_____

Which individuals are most likely to describe you accurately, honestly, and passionately?

_____

_____

_____

_____

_____

Which individuals think they know you the best, but actually know you the least?

_____

_____

_____

_____

_____

What is the most common thing that almost everyone knows about you and would describe fairly accurately?

_____

_____

_____

_____

_____

Influential Real, Historical, or Fictional Persons

- Family members, friends, teachers, or others who have most influenced your life
- Historical or fictional individuals who have inspired thoughts and feelings
- Individuals deserving of more praise and recognition than they typically receive
- Individuals who have significantly contributed to your academic and intellectual development
- Individuals who have significantly contributed to your personal and emotional development
- Real, historical, or fictional individuals who inspire the most questions or curiosity within you

What would you like these individuals to know about you?

_____

_____

_____

_____

What would you like to know about these individuals?

_____

_____

_____

_____

Which individuals should be told how much they mean to you, and why?

_____

_____

_____

_____

Which individuals will never learn how much they mean to you?

_____

_____

_____

_____

_____

_____

_____

What characteristics or qualities do real or fictional individuals who have influenced your life share?

_____

_____

_____

_____

_____

_____

Life Experiences

- Comical situations that you remember or that someone has told you about
- Meaningful experiences that involved you, friends, or family
- Experiences you most often share with others
- Experiences you least often share with others
- Experiences you have never discussed with others
- Embarrassing experiences you would like family to stop sharing with others
- Those experiences that have most impacted your thoughts, feelings, and actions to date
- Those experiences that you would like to happen, but haven't yet

Which experiences would you like others to know about, but you have not yet shared?

_____

_____

_____

_____

_____

_____

With which individuals have you shared the most meaningful experiences?

_____

_____

_____

_____

_____

Which experiences would reveal the most about you to people who have never met you?

_____

_____

_____

_____

Which experiences have had subtle, yet meaningful or profound influences on your thoughts about college?

_____

_____

_____

_____

Which experiences have had subtle, yet meaningful or profound influences on your thoughts about life?

_____

_____

_____

_____

_____

Quotations

- Quotations you recall vaguely or thoroughly from memory
- Quotations you look up in a book or on the Web
- Silliest quotation that you like the most
- Smartest quotation that you don't quite understand,
  though it moves you to think
- Quotations that have been used as essay questions before
- Quotations you would like to use in essays now

What, inspired by phrases in quotations or the subject matter
of quotations, would you like others to know about you?

_____

_____

_____

_____

How or what do the individuals who spoke the quotations, or
the circumstances surrounding these quotations, make you
think or feel?

_____

_____

_____

_____

What keyword or three-word phrase is most significant within the quotation?

_____

What subject area do you find most appealing when you review a book of quotations?

_____

Which songwriters, poets, authors, or celebrities would you like to be able to quote at will?

_____

_____

_____

_____

_____

Travel or Life Overseas

- Places you have lived or visited in the United States or abroad
- Places where you would like to live or visit in the United States or abroad
- Most significant travel or relocation experience
- Objects you travel with (including teddy bears)
- Books, movies, or television productions about other lands, people, or cultures that have inspired you

Which travel, relocation, or overseas living experience has inspired the most questions?

_____

_____

_____

_____

_____

Which travel, relocation, or overseas living experience has inspired the most vivid memories?

_____

_____

_____

_____

_____

Who shared these experiences with you, and would their thoughts be different?

_____

_____

_____

_____

_____

What places are on your list of those you must visit someday, and why?

_____

_____

_____

_____

Risks

- Definition of risk
- Events others would agree were risky
- Events only you would characterize as risky
- Lessons learned vicariously by observation or by interactions with others taking risks
- Risks you have read about in literature or in the news that inspired you intellectually and emotionally
- Risks that yielded negative results and those that yielded positive results

What would you like others to know about you as a risk taker?

_____

_____

_____

_____

_____

_____

What circumstances most inspire risky actions or support taking risks?

_____

_____

_____

_____

_____

Which individuals do you define as risk takers? How have they influenced you the most?

_____

_____

_____

_____

_____

What risks did you not take that you now wish you did?

_____

_____

_____

_____

What risks that you or others took yielded the largest rewards?

_____

_____

_____

_____

_____

_____

_____

Science, Technology, and Discoveries

- Self-proclaimed "geek" or "science aficionado"
- Historical advancements or discoveries that are most impressive
- Recent advancements or discoveries that are most impressive
- Characteristics you believe are required to stimulate scientific, technological, or related discoveries
- Necessities that served as the mothers of invention or, at least, creative thinking
- Individuals you have met who are most likely to invent or discover something
- Discoveries you would have liked to have made or those you will someday make
- Most significant scientific or technical activities you have been involved in

Which areas of science and technology are of particular academic interest?

_____

Which areas of science and technology are of general human interest?

_____

Which science fiction–based activity, capability, object, or resource would you like to become everyday fact?

_____

Which stereotype of "the science guy/gal" do you most resemble and least resemble?

_____
_____
_____

What do you love or hate about science or technology?

_____
_____
_____
_____
_____
_____

Sports

- Sports you compete in at a varsity level and those you participate in for fun
- Sports you follow as a fanatic, not just fan
- Lessons learned on the court, field, or in the pool
- Characteristics you most admire in others who compete or participate in sports
- World-class competitors who demonstrate qualities you admire
- Most admired friend or family member who competes or participates in sports
- Most admired professionals or amateurs involved in your favorite event/sport
- Sports-related fantasies that are attainable and those that are just dreams

What would you like others to know about the impact sports have had on you?

_____

_____

_____

_____

_____

What would teammates or coaches say about how sports have influenced you, and how you have influenced others as a result?

_____

_____

_____

_____

_____

What feelings or thoughts about sports have you never shared with others?

_____

_____

_____

_____

_____

Which sports-related figures embody philosophies you believe in?

_____

_____

_____

_____

_____

_____

What would be the most surprising thing for others to learn about your involvement with sports?

_____

_____

_____

_____

_____

Values and Philosophies

- Actual circumstances generating moral dilemmas and values clarification
- People you consider philosophers who might surprise others if they knew
- Concerns about values and moral issues
- Words that reflect intellectual, emotional, and life philosophies
- Philosophies and values that will serve you well as you enter college
- Philosophies and values that might cause some concerns as you enter college

What are values and philosophies that friends and family would be surprised to hear you express?

_____

_____

_____

_____

_____

_____

_____

_____

_____

_____

What do you value the most and least?

_____

_____

_____

_____

_____

_____

_____

_____

What circumstances most impacted your establishing certain values and philosophies?

_____

_____

_____

_____

_____

_____

_____

What deep philosophical beliefs would you like to share, but you haven't had the opportunity to do so?

_____

_____

_____

_____

_____

_____

_____

By now, you should realize that there is really nothing to fear but fear itself. Hey, that could be an inspirational quote offered within an essay question (and it has been). The unknown generates anxiety. Familiarity yields comfort and confidence. Gradually we are demystifying the unknown and, we hope, enhancing your confidence. By the time you finish this book you will know how to write essays that will be more than just answers to questions from a content perspective, addressing specific issues and making impassioned arguments. They will be the best self-reflective word pictures you can paint for others to see. They will be expressions of what you truly want to reveal, not just guesses about what you think others want to see. They will truly be "you-nique" and powerful essays.

So far you have learned about the process of admissions essay writing and issues related to general essay writing. You have become familiar with the six easy-to-follow steps to essay writing success and have begun the initial self-assessment and brainstorming steps. In the next few chapters you will learn the drafting, editing, and finalizing steps by studying sample essays with summary analyses for each. The Before-and-After Review and Comprehensive Critique will reveal what it would be like if you had your own personal essay coach, and you will learn "critiquing guidelines" to utilize on your own drafts.

We realize that by now you should be really, really, really ready to begin drafting your own documents, but please keep reading before you do.

The next few chapters will reveal how you can complete the last three of the six steps to essay writing success. You will have the opportunity to review essay samples and summary analyses offered by contributors. As you read these essays and comments, you will see what to look for when transforming first drafts into second drafts and second drafts into finished works. Also, you will review a before-and-after transformation that will show you how an essay progresses to an improved version by addressing key points. A comprehensive narrative critique will allow you to "eavesdrop" on a hypothetical exchange between the essay writer and a personal essay coach who sounds surprisingly like the common voice of author and contributors (what a coincidence!). Continue reading, and soon you will begin writing, editing, and finalizing great essays that you'll send off to schools with confidence!

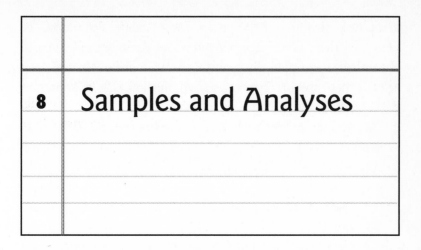

8 | Samples and Analyses

AT FIRST, WE PLANNED to include "good, bad, and ugly" examples in this book. Thank goodness, as writing progressed, logic and positive thinking prevailed. All essays are, sincerely, illustrations of writing talents, revelations of thoughts, and reflections of feelings. There are no bad or ugly essays, only some that are better than others. Tips and strategies offered by this book will ensure that your essays will have maximum impact on your candidacy. The samples and comments that follow will, in positive ways, inspire your writing efforts.

When you review essays written by actual candidates very much like you, please focus on what you have done and what you will do, not on the achievements of others. The individuals who wrote these essays are not your "competition." Their writing prowess and hypothetical admissions potential is not better than yours. While some essays document interesting experiences, the truth is that you can do the same. These samples should generate the inspiration of confidence, not the perspiration that arises from unfounded anxiety. If you follow the steps outlined in this book, your essays will be as good as, if not better than, those in this chapter.

While references to particular schools do appear, in order to add needed context to some samples, no essayist names are associated with any of the pieces. Earlier, in the dedication, we identified those who cared enough about candidates like you to share their works publicly. In truth, the willingness to reveal one's self to others, specifically admissions professionals, is an important psychological step for all essay writers.

As you review these select essays, utilize the criteria first presented in Chapter 6 to analyze each piece. Ask and answer the following questions for all samples presented:

- Did the essayist respond directly or creatively to the essay question?
- Do the details offered in each supporting body paragraph support the introductory paragraph and, specifically, the essay's topic sentence?
- Did the essayist follow an obvious order, appear logical, and flow to a conclusion?
- Did the essayist project a consistent and active voice, and follow grammar and structure guidelines?
- Did the essayist use vocabulary that is appropriate, clear, concise, and focused?
- Does the essay reveal the essayist's personality, values, interests, and hopes?
- Does the essayist reveal knowledge of the school or of special circumstances related to his or her candidacy?
- Could the essayist have omitted sentences, used alternative words, or reordered sentence presentations?
- Is each sentence clear and necessary, serving the purposes of each paragraph and of the entire essay?

Later, when you draft your own pieces, you will ask these questions again, as first-person inquiries. Then, your answers will determine whether you have revisions remaining or are finished and ready to submit your essays to target schools.

Also, when you read each sample, think about how these essayists addressed general themes and particular questions. Specifically, which of these themes, which first appeared in Chapter 7, apply to each piece?

- Accomplishments and pride
- Activities and interests
- Art, drama, and music
- Autobiographical self-portraits
- Careers and ambitions
- College academics and college life
- Current events and world issues
- Dilemmas, ethics, and morals
- Disappointments and failures
- Diversity
- Family and friends
- Influential real, historical, or fictional persons
- Life experiences
- Quotations
- Travel or life overseas
- Risks
- Science, technology, and discoveries
- Sports
- Values and philosophies

After you read the essays and identify multiple themes that apply to each, you will see how various ideas can be used to address any number of school inquiries. You will realize that you have the freedom to focus on feelings and themes that sincerely interest you and truly reveal who you are as an individual. Application questions should empower and inspire you, not limit or frustrate you. These samples will help you understand what I mean.

Sample One

I was born in college—delivered on March 7, 1983, in a university hospital in a college town. The school could be seen out my window of my hospital room, and two university employees, my parents, were there to welcome me. I was immediately immersed into the world of academia. I lived in campus housing; my favorite babysitters were college students; and I breathed college air at lectures, concerts, and countless basketball, football, and hockey games. Now, looking back at my childhood, I feel as if I'm coming full circle. I hope I'll have a unique perspective to share with those who will teach me and learn from me.

For thirteen of my seventeen years, I have followed my father on his career path, learning the true meaning of "student life" on a variety of campuses. As I grew up, college was where my role models lived, where my friends and I swam year-round, and where fun was to be had. Having visited numerous campuses in my junior and senior years, I took many, many campus tours, attended many, many information sessions and, usually heard many—too many—of the same questions asked over and over by anxious students and parents. I always listened to the responses of the campus representative with my ears, as well as my heart. It was with the acute sensitivities of a child born and raised in college that I listened to the ways in which a particular school might become my home and, in time, a place that I would return as an alumna.

I have had many unique experiences, and I have lived in a variety of different zip codes. Penn will provide the diverse environment I seek, a nurturing and eclectic place that will assuredly feel like home to me. The Penn representatives, students, and alumni I have met in recent months, as well as my father's own recounted memories, echo this sense of "Penn as home." During experiences throughout my life I have concluded that college is a community of thought and growth that challenges your mind as well as your spirit. When I enter as a freshman, I want to recreate those experiences, on a first-person basis. I want to have adventures, make friends, and learn things that will stay with me permanently.

I already have a passion for college life, and I want to get the most out of every experience. I will walk on campus in the fall carrying a vast array of opinions and ideas about college, and I will spend each of my four years exploring and learning through others their validity. For the next four years, in the world of the Palestra, Super Block, Franklin Field, and WaWas, I will find out whether I'm destined to learn more in the classroom or beyond.

- 468 words
- 4 paragraphs
- Response to specific query: "What characteristics of Penn, and yourself, make the University a particularly good match for you? Briefly describe how you envision your first year in college. How will your presence be known on campus?"
- Combination of direct and creative response to posed question
- Began biographical, flowed to philosophical, revealing personal views about and expectations concerning the college experience
- Ended with school-specific references
- Smooth transition between paragraphs using logical and obvious order
- Can "hear" writer's voice throughout; doesn't use flowery or excessive language
- Third paragraph is especially helpful in providing sense of wants and ideals of the writer

- Obvious knowledge of school to which she is applying as evinced by detailed info
- Would you have included discussions of meaningful secondary cocurricular or academics?
- Would you have focused on a particular personal quality to share with readers?
- Would you have provided more information about first-year academics, cocurricular, or relationships?

Sample Two

I was a reluctant nomad. Fate, fueled by my father's career ambition, has moved me to different houses, six different states, and two different coasts. I have learned to live without constants and take advantage of chance. With each new environment, I try to adapt and conform, sometimes even to rebel. The adjustments are tedious, though with time they hurt less and come more easily. I have mastered the art of nesting. The sturdy nest, the hard-won skills have never, however, kept me in my home. I am still and forever at the will of circumstance.

When I was seven, my family moved from Princeton, New Jersey, to Stockton, California. I doubt you could find any two places less alike than these are. I found myself inundated with foreign accents, foreign lifestyles, and foreign temperatures. I approached this new environment with the same technique I had learned to use in other moves. I quickly immersed myself in the culture of my new home. I became familiar with my surroundings, built up a year-round summer wardrobe, and learned to pepper my speech with "like" and "totally." I became the ultimate "California girl." It was not an easy task. I would always have brown hair and would always be bound to my Eastern Standard roots. With time, though, the sun lightened a few strands of my hair, and I exchanged my memories of the icy Eastern seaboard for the waters of the warm Pacific. California became my home.

Fate had taken me to the Golden State, and I was determined to become a native. I spent my days in a one-story, open-air public school. I practiced earthquake drills, learned the name and history of every Spanish mission, and took field trips to gold-rush towns. I joined a swim team and practiced year-round in an outdoor pool. I ate granola and conserved water. I became accustomed to the rarely changing weather patterns. California was no longer a Hollywood cliché, but was now the source of my ethics and values. West Coast mentality had been successfully embedded deep in my soul. But this depth mattered not when fate, once again, stepped in and sent me clear across the country to Rochester, New York.

I could still be a Californian, but now I had to do it from three thousand miles away. The summer after my freshman year in high school, eight years after our arrival in California, my family packed our things and relocated to upstate New York. My successful efforts to live as a Californian now made me an outcast. I was living in a new city among people and weather conditions drastically different than what I was accustomed to. Life as I knew it ceased to exist. In school, I knew too much about westward expansion and too little about the geography of New England. The only nearby beach was adjacent to a lake: no shells, no tides, no surfers. Swim practice now meant spending two hours in a hot, humid dome that smelled potently of chlorine. Everything I defined myself by now seemed useless and out of style. I had spent eight years of my life embracing the ideals of western mentality, only to find myself back on eastern soil. I have spent countless hours of my seventeen years adjusting to my surroundings.

With each move, after a little mourning and some complaining, I ultimately have chosen to become a part of each new address. I have loved many houses, I have loathed others, never have I chosen how long they will be mine. Posters are taped, not nailed to temporary walls. In the dorms or apartments of my college, this will be the celebratory norm, not a sad fact to face. Books and inspirational speakers may tell you that you can direct your life and map out a path toward success. But, ultimately, you will never be able to predict the twists, the turns, and the surprises of life. The country is vast, the authority figures inscrutable, and the moving vans abundant. You can pack the boxes, and develop the soul that will travel, but in the end you're just along for the ride.

- 694 words
- 5 paragraphs
- Response to specific query: "You have just completed your 300-page autobiography. Please submit page 217."
- Biographical piece revealed ability to adapt to new circumstances, sensitivities to differences of others, constancy of cocurricular involvement, and a vision for the future
- Introductory paragraph keeps the reader wanting more; great support for following paragraphs
- Excellent example of how the essayist can "show rather than tell" as reader is taken on a virtual road map from coast to coast, exposing us to various sounds, tastes, and cultural adjustments
- Would the essayist be an interesting roommate to live with and learn from?
- Would you have taken the closing sentiments a bit further, adding a new sentence projecting expectations of college life or future goals as part of "the ride"?
- Would you have added a sentence or two addressing the "celebratory norms" of college life and how they match this essayist's personality?
- Would you have added some school-specific references to what might be involved in "the ride" or "celebratory norms" at particular schools?
- What did you learn about the essayist as you read this piece?

Sample Three

He called it his Greenwood tree, a tall white pine that towered above his neighborhood across from the railroad tracks. The town wanted to cut it down, but he wouldn't hear of it. He said he liked to believe that it had been planted before his birth, which would have made it nearly one hundred

Arthur was 96, the youngest son of a former slave from South Carolina. He was the fourteenth child in his family and during his long life he had worked as a locksmith, a tailor, a barber, an artist, a coal miner and a Baptist minister. When I met him, Arthur was working as a gardener, a man who seemed to me to have a magical touch on the outdoors.

Each Tuesday morning at 4:30am I would wake up to his whistle outside my bedroom window. I don't know how he saw his way around in the dark, but he did. And as I lay listening in my warm bed, he would eventually break into a spiritual song. He called it his work music.

He wore rubber bands around the bottom of his pant legs to keep the ticks away. On his head he wore an old leather hat which he never removed. As early as I can remember I worked at Arthur's side. The first lesson he ever taught me was how to get leaves off a rake when they were stuck. He showed me how to turn the rake upside down and then pull backward across the grass. He taught me how to edge the lawn and transplant, how to properly chop kindling, mend a stone wall, and how to break up rock outcroppings with a sledge hammer. He taught me to be patient, explaining that no job was too small. Without my realizing it, during the fifteen years of your friendship, he taught me lessons about life and death and honesty and about what really matters. Every day that we were together, he preached the benefits of a simple, humble lifestyle.

During the cold months Arthur did not work. And each Christmas eve we had a tradition of visiting him. I was always nervous going into his dark house. I preferred seeing him outside. Inside he seemed smaller and I barely recognized him without his hat. His head was almost bald. He lived with his wife, Lucille, who had suffered a stroke. She could not use her hands very well but she would motion for me to sit next to her and I remember always being scared. I remember once asking Arthur why he did not have a Christmas tree. He took me outside to his porch, which was falling apart, and he pointed to his Greenwood tree. "There's my tree" he said proudly.

After Lucille died, Arthur aged quickly. His cloths were often dirty. His buttons or zipper left open. He stopped brushing his teeth and grew increasingly forgetful. Once he arrived to work at 2:30 in the morning, unaware that it was the middle of the night. His edging along the border of the lawn was not longer as straight and tight. Once I found him asleep, sitting against a tree. And then one day he too suffered a stroke. When we visited him in the hospital, I told Arthur that while he was sick I would keep the land in shape. As I worked, I convinced myself that Arthur would be back and how proud he would be to see what I'd done. But, he never did return. The day he died I worked outside all day long and into the evening, my mind spinning.

Recently I drove past Arthur's house and noticed that the Greenwood Tree had been cut down. A new family sat on his rickety front porch. As I drove home I listened to his early morning work music echo inside my head. It was a song of my friend and teacher—a teacher who taught much more than just gardening. It was the song of a very simple and decent life that helped shape who I was to become.

- 683 words
- 7 paragraphs
- Addresses topics related to persons who impacted one's life, lessons learned from others, and diversity

- Could also be response to requests for autobiographical or self-portrait pieces
- Through narrative describing another, the essayist revealed much about sensitivities to age, race, socio-economic status, values, and personal growth
- Excellent imagery, beautiful recounting of an individual who had a profound impact on the essayist's life
- Offers insight into the writer's values, morals, sense of attitude toward diverse individuals
- Sincere, honest representation of self
- Would you have used a school-specific reference at the end, such as: "As I walk down the tree-lined pathway toward (insert name of building on school campus), I will listen for this song within my heart, and seek to find faculty, scholars, and friends who can teach me and shape me as much as Arthur"?
- Would you have more overtly addressed what can be learned from people who personify diversity?
- What did you learn about the essayist as you read this piece?

Sample Four

A placid cheesy surface, a tantalizing aroma of tomato sauce and pepperoni a delectable texture of light, fluffy crust—underneath all this lies a hidden danger, one of which even those who deliver it are unaware. It conceals itself within every square inch of this seemingly harmless treat, a clandestine terror waiting for its target to let its guard down and take a big bite of the steaming greasy goodness. As the victim luxuriates in the luscious, warm delicacy, it is too late; the damage has been done, the victim, guilty of nothing but hunger, has already fallen prey to the peril of pizza. This danger is . . . phenylalanine. Yes, that's right, a common household amino acid gone bad!

As entertaining a Fox Television special as that would make, it is partially true. I am lucky enough to have a heritable metabolic disorder known as phenylketonuria, or PKU. This means that I lack a specific enzyme, phenylalanine hydroxylase. This enzyme normally converts the amino acid phenylalanine, found in almost all protein containing foods including pizza, into another amino acid, tyrosine. Phenylalanine is a neurotoxin in high concentrations, so this mechanism is vital. If left untreated, PKU results in mental retardation due to buildup of phenylalanine. Since I was diagnosed an infant, I have had no problems. True, I can't eat the majority of foods that contain these proteins but I am pretty lucky. I will live a "normal' life if I follow my eating restrictions and continue to take my dietary supplements.

Many see this as a hard life. Oftentimes, I am asked if I am angry at my parents for passing this apparent curse on to me, or at my sister for not sharing in my supposed misery. Of course I am not angry with them—it's not as if my mom and dad found out they were having another bundle of joy, they told the doctor they wanted desperately to make his life as hard as possible by not letting him eat anything. My restrictions have never really been too hard for me, it's just something with which I live. Yes, I have to remember not to eat many foods that are usually childhood dietary staples. However, all that did was require me to remember a few things that "normal" kids don't have to remember. It forced me to mature at an early age and take responsibility for myself—there are fates worse than discipline.

The biggest food hassle that I can remember was that I couldn't have as many M&Ms as the other kids at my class holiday parties in elementary school. Since I did not build my self-confidence or self-image on my M&M eating prowess, I managed to survive that ordeal. By far, the most annoying side effect of my PKU is the sign I seem to wear on my back saying

"Pity me, PLEASE!" I don't mind explaining to people why I only order a salad at the best steak restaurant in the DC Metro area, honestly I don't. Sometimes, though, I wish I could just tell everyone I know, have known, and will ever know to gather in one place at one time so I only have to explain it once. It's not the explaining I mind, it's the reaction I receive that really irks me.

Any guy I talk to tells me without fail that I'm not missing anything and that whatever he happens to be eating isn't really that good anyway. It's like I'm five and he's trying to stop me from crying by insisting that Santa Claus really does exist—somewhat insulting. Any girl I speak with always gives me the sad eyes and the classic "awwwww", as if a three-legged puppy was being fed by its two-legged mother. PKU can be debilitating if left untreated—this much is true. However, my PKU is being treated. When I am pitied, I feel less than human. I feel like I'm that three-legged puppy. Instead of debilitated, I prefer to think of myself more as . . . a genetically mandated extreme vegetarian.

When I wrote I was lucky enough to have PKU, I was only being partially facetious. My diet may be fairly limited, but the number of adults that have responded to my explanation by telling me that they wish that they couldn't eat half of the trash they put in their body is astronomical. While the health benefits are nice, the most important thing PKU has given me is my biological curiosity. As a five year old, I noticed that I couldn't eat certain foods, but didn't know why. I needed to know why I was different from the rest of my friends. To this end, I asked question after question of anyone who would stand still long enough to listen and whom I thought to be knowledgeable. I asked my parents, my friends' parents, and my teachers—literally any adult I could find. I eventually discovered that I had PKU, a metabolic disorder caused by something called my genes. Of course, I then had to know what metabolic meant and what genes were, so I started being a pest again. The more I learned, the more I found I didn't know.

This cycle continued to repeat itself and still does today. My questions regarding my eating habits has transformed into a full-fledged precocious biological curiosity. This curiosity led me to apply for an internship at the National Institute of Health, an opportunity traditionally open to no one younger than a college undergraduate. However, I was selected and was lucky enough to spend eight weeks learning about genetics and running mutation analyses for rare disease patients under Dr. Bill Gahl at the National Human Genome Research Institute. Through this experience, I have decided that clinical genetic research is a very possible career option for me—an uncommon and rather invaluable realization.

My PKU may have denied me the consolation of ice cream after a rocky end to a relationship, and I might not be able to eat much when I get my wisdom teeth out since I cannot eat frozen yogurt, but it has shaped who I am and who I want to be. That beats the Killer Pizza any day of the week.

- 1,044 words
- 8 paragraphs
- Addresses topics associated with challenges, overcoming adversity, philosophies, and, possibly, career goals
- Self-portrait revealed personal qualities, interest in science, as well as a special sense of self
- Great, catchy opening, nice use of subtle but appropriate humor, quirky, cute
- Excellent use of personal experiences to give validity to possible career interests
- Included internship experience in a way that fits in nicely with rest of the essay

- Doesn't use adversity to gain sympathy but rather to discuss what was learned from an illness and how these lessons will be applied in the future
- Reader learns how the student deals with difficult situations and can gather insight as to how the author would deal with other challenges in life
- Would you have shortened the piece? If yes, how?
- What would you have titled this piece to enhance reader curiosity and project a sense of wit?
- Would you have expanded upon the impact this life circumstance had on an interest in science, research, and medicine?
- What else would you have liked to know about the essayist, and how could that information be included in this piece?

Sample Five

A gust of damp, hot air greeted my skin when I entered the room. The fan, in its futile effort to cool the sweltering room, accomplished no purpose other than rustling the strewn pages of "Pakistan National News" and causing the bed linen to shiver. I flung myself down on the sofa, and heaving a sigh of resignation opened to the first chapter of my summer reading novel, *A Thousand Acres*. As I half-heartedly scanned the pages, my gaze drifted over to the servant girl working in the room. Beads of perspiration dipped unnoticed down her temples and the scarf draped over her head clung wearily to her neck, only adding to the feeling of being suffocated by the humid heat. The warmth did not seem to affect me as much as it did her, but then, I lounged beneath a ceiling fan. She crouched low on the floor in a crab-like position, vigorously sweeping the floor with a hand-made broom of pine needles bound together by a copper cord. Her expression appeared stoic and her movement robotic. For an instant her eyes rose to meet mine, and I saw I had been mistaken. The complacency, even indifference, I thought I had seen, belied her true emotions: longing and envy. "You can read?" she asked suddenly, her voice a barely audible murmur, a curious mix of disbelief, awe and jealousy.

I do not recall how I responded, but I do remember that in that instant it occurred to me how similar this young girl and I were in appearance. She and I shared the same thick, black hair, dark eyes, olive complexion. Full lips and even the slight dimples on our right cheeks matched. But there were unavoidable differences. We both wore a shalvar and kamis, the typical garb of a Pakistani Muslim, but my attire was new and freshly laundered, while hers was a shabby, threadbare hand-me-down. I reclined on a plush sofa in my grandfather's home in Pakistan, lolling in the relaxation and luxury of what I considered a well-deserved summer vacation from a rigorous academic schedule. Meanwhile, this young girl barely sixteen, labored as a maid in my grandfather's house, a coveted and lucrative occupation for a girl from an impoverished village. It struck me, she and I shared identical smiles, nationalities and faiths, yet she stood on the outside, longingly watching me seize the endless stream of opportunities that came my way. Sheer circumstance separated this girl from myself.

Moments before I had been bemoaning the task of summer reading, yet this illiterate and destitute servant girl did not see it as a cumbersome chore, but rather as a gift. The moment left me ashamed of my self-absorbed ignorance. The guilt faded and then came the recognition of the invaluable truth my "reflection" had shown me. Middle-class status, the comfort of a home, literacy and an education are privileges, or blessings, if you like, rather than self-evident, deserved rights. Thus, it is my duty to maximize these opportunities and daily acknowledge my fortunate lifestyle.

In a moment of impetuosity I asked the young girl if she would like to take a look at the cover of the novel. She hesitated, and then with a shy nod came over and tentatively crouched beside the sofa. I motioned for her to sit beside me. Again she approached timidly, glancing consciously down at her stained cloths. I smiled, noting that she seemed visibly reassured by the affable gesture. She intently scrutinized the pages, fingering with the utmost of care and reverence, I sat beside her, offering explanations as to the plot. We sat shoulder-to-shoulder, side-by-side.

- 606 words
- 3 paragraphs
- Addresses requests for self-portraits and topics related to autobiographic reflections or family
- Narrative about an event reveals insights into self, understanding of class differences, and an altruistic quality
- Uses imagery to engage the reader, allowing reader to witness and feel everything the essayist witnessed and felt
- Says so much about the writer without specifically spelling things out; the subtleties work very well
- Reveals how privileged opportunities and way of life yield a wonderful learning experience and life-altering event
- Snapshot approach works well here; takes one moment, one brief instant, and illustrates it for the reader clearly, concisely, and profoundly
- Would you have added a concluding paragraph containing references to "teachable moments," projecting how much the essayist wishes to learn in college, and how much the essayist wishes to share with others?
- Would you have made reference to how the essayist's cultural heritage and the images shared in this piece motivate this candidate to strive for academic achievements?

- Would you have expanded upon the statement, "Thus, it is my duty to maximize these opportunities and daily acknowledge my fortunate lifestyle," perhaps with an additional paragraph built upon this idea?

Sample Six

My family history is mysterious. I grew up hearing stories about an escape from Myanmar during the Japanese invasion, then flight from Lahore during the turbulent India-Pakistan partition. Yet these stories mattered little, for I had made my own difficult journeys from continent to continent. The past remained irrelevant since I was never able to relate to it. However, in the winter of 2001 I finally realized the connection between past, present and future, for that was when I visited the place where it all began: Monwa, Myanmar.

The trip to Monwa was a tedious five hours on an unkempt road. Yet that mattered little, as the destination was the home of my triple-great grandparents, the origin of our family stories. We arrived not knowing where to go or whom to meet since none of us had ever been to Myanmar, let alone to a farming village that had been open to foreigners for only five years. My father believed it hopeless to inquire about a family that had dwelt here four generations ago. Yet, something compelled us to continue, leading us to an old Sikh temple withering from years of use.

I entered alongside my parents wearing Levi Jeans, frazzled from the long ride, thinking only of the Hyatt. My father spoke in his native tongue, Punjabi, a language linked to Hindi. We expected nothing to come of his conversation, but to our astonishment our family name had not been forgotten. An elder announced that remains of the Jollys could still be found in Monwa. A girl then brought out a giant brass vessel with the engraving "thekedar JoIly," meaning "Jolly the constructor." My triple great-grandfather had donated this vessel in the early 1900s. At that time, he was known as "the constructor" since he had built the roads around Monwa. The elder also informed us that the house of my forefather remained standing, though in ruins after the Japanese bombings. He then showed us the way to the home of my ancestors.

When we arrived, our first glimpse was of a staircase leading nowhere, yet through the dust and decay the remnants of a grand mansion were still visible. The ruins' high ceilings, meticulous wall carvings, and large rooms hinted of the house's past splendor. Tears welled as I idealized that a near century ago my relatives dwelt here, discussing their futures under this roof. Outside was a single well, which had provided the water for the dwellers and the hundreds of acres of farmland. Nowadays it remained stagnant since chemicals from the bombings had seeped into it. The history of the land was as astounding as that of my family.

The trip to Monwa changed me. Somehow the past became more than bedtime stories. The torments and distress of leaving everything behind was something I had become accustomed to, but in Monwa I realized that each generation of my family since the migration from Myanmar shared this experience. We all had faced obstacles of different sorts, and every generation had risen victoriously with only memories as scars. I too would soon embark on my own adventure, but now, I feared not this journey, since I knew that the watchful eyes of my ancestors would never leave my side.

- 541 words
- 5 paragraphs
- Addresses topics associated with family, cultural heritage, and meaningful events

- Reflections on a particular event revealed a sense of self and history
- Essayist experienced growth and shares this with the reader, alluding that perhaps this journey has prepared her for the challenges of college
- Would you like to know more about how this experience changed the essayist and how it impacted future experiences?
- Would you have expanded upon the impact of this experience, and connected it with academic, community service, or career goals?
- Would you have connected the essayist's past to future desires and present motivations by adding a sixth and closing paragraph, building upon the essay's topic sentence "past, present, and future" theme and on the "adventure" of college?
- What would your new closing paragraph contain?

Sample Seven

As Pythagoras was walking down a path one fine Greek morning, his ears took note of a unique sound made by a blacksmith striking two pieces of iron simultaneously. Each anvil yielded a difference sound. Each had a different pitch, a different timbre, and a different resonance. However, they sounded pleasant when struck together, and Pythagoras was set to determine the nature of this aural phenomenon.

Pythagoras was already a well-established mathematician. He had devised theorems and postulates, many of which are essential to trigonometry and conceptual physics today. By virtue of his vast knowledge of mathematical concepts, Pythagoras used his observations to develop a theory to explain the remarkable, yet peculiar accordance between the two different sounds. He developed a mathematical system that served as the basis for present-day musical theory. In his lifetime, Pythagoras advanced the study of both music and mathematics. I would like to follow his lead, using the mastery of each discipline as a complement to the other.

As a student of both the School of Music and the Mellon College of Science, I will be able to study and learn more about my two passions. Furthermore, I will be able to study the relationship between both fields, and perhaps discover new patterns between them and new ways in which they relate. Being a student in the BSA program will help me fulfill my dream of being a modern-day Pythagoras.

- 236 words
- 3 paragraphs
- Addresses specific queries associated with "why this school" or "this program" as well as themes related to influential historical figures, academic focus, and career curiosity
- Specific response as short-answer essay, reveals a sense of history and a sense of self, as well as a unique set of academic interests.
- Provides reader with clear understanding of interests and academic goals of the writer
- Clearly written for a very specific purpose for a specific kind of school/program
- Essayist uses a creative approach to capture the reader's interest while answering the question concisely
- Essayist clearly understands and cares about the subject of the essay
- Would you have expanded a bit more on particular academic and career goals?
- Would you have elaborated on the essayist's stated "dream" and revealed more about what a "modern-day Pythagoras" would do?

Sample Eight

I have been in the presence of genius. It was June of 2002 and I was sitting in what was quite possibly the worst seat of a very crowded auditorium. I sat and waited for a man I knew intimately, but had never met. My stomach was knotted with excitement at the prospect of finally seeing, in person, someone whose work I had admired ever since I had first listened to it seven years earlier. I'd never even heard him speak, but through his musical voice and his beautifully crafted lyrics, Stephen Sondheim had touched every aspect of my life and had become my greatest role model.

The musical and intellectual giant finally emerged from the wings looking tiny in comparison to the expansive stage. Frustrated by the tears that were blurring my first sight of him, I rose to my feet, clapping and yelling along with several hundred other fans. Eventually the commotion died down and the interview began. I sat on the edge of my seat, opera glasses firmly pressed to my face. Mr. Sondheim spoke and I soaked up every word. He was everything that his music had suggested he would be. He was witty, sensitive, introspective, and educated. Listening to him opened my eyes up to why I admire him and what my admiration of him says about who I am.

Stephen Sondheim is my role model because he is an educated man who puts all of himself into the music he writes. He has worked hard and studied music all his life and that is why he has the ability to write such beautiful and poignant music. My goal is to become the best singer I can be. I use Stephen Sondheim's example of hard work and perseverance to keep me going, even when my goals seem extremely remote. I am inspired by Sondheim as a musician, certainly, but he is my role model beyond the world of music. When I heard his interview I realized that what makes Stephen Sondheim truly great at what he does, is that fact that he is a well-educated and extremely informed individual. He is someone who took an active role in his own education and for that reason turned out to be one of the most intellectual and eloquent people of our time. Like my role model, I am taking an active part. In applying to the New England Conservatory, I am choosing a place that will bring me closer to my goal of being a great musician and great intellectual as well.

I view my life as a quest to fulfill all my potential. I have already come a long way in my quest, and I still have far to go. Stephen Sondheim's example has helped me immensely up to this point, and it was in following his example that I determined that the New England Conservatory is the place where I will receive the finest training as a musician and as a reading, thinking, and caring human being.

- 502 words
- 4 paragraphs
- Short-answer essay for a very specific school—a conservatory of music—addressing issues related to influential individuals, role models, and significant music-related life events
- Essayist's interest is obviously sincere and grounded from past experiences
- Writer shares one moment of the past in order to project future goals, plans, and aspirations
- Admits that she doesn't know it all, writing, "I still have far to go"; expresses a degree of humility and a desire to learn and grow more
- School-specific reference is sincere and appropriate in tone
- Would you have expanded a bit more on music-focused academic and career goals, elaborating upon what being "a great musician and great intellectual" means?
- Would you have highlighted particular course titles and academic topics or added references to particular faculty and their specialties?
- Would you want to learn more about the Sondheim-like qualities and curiosities this essayist possesses?

Sample Nine

I have always dreaded the words, "What kind of music do you like?" Time and time again, people have asked me this question in a friendly attempt to make small talk, or perhaps to break a silence in an awkward conversation, While their intentions may have been honest, they never realized the anxious wreck I became while trying to stutter a coherent answer.

Until recently, I never found myself able to proudly respond with "Classical, how about you?" I knew this answer would generate a blank look and the possible raising of an eyebrow. Instead, I would say "Don't really have a favorite. I like all kinds," and then picture Mozart shaking his head at me. Not only was I self-conscious about my taste of music, but I knew I would have to explain myself at length about the nature of my preference, unusual for a teenage boy.

How could I possibly describe the sheer ecstasy I feel when hearing a coloratura soprano gliding her way through the "Queen of the Night" aria from Mozart's *Die Zauberflot*, hitting each high F gloriously and precisely, while a 35-piece orchestra supports her with Mozart's brilliant symphony, shifting from minor to major key, while still retaining the breathtaking tempo of perpetual eight notes? The music of Mozart's grandiose operas is only matched by his delightful piano sonatas, whose delicate scales and cadences define perfect music. Nobody could possibly understand how the last movement of Beethoven's *Pastorale* symphony overwhelms me with its simple, yet majestic melody, repeating itself through crescendos, building toward an exhilarating climax, only to resolve with one final echo of the mode, played by the soft tone of a solo French horn. The sensation I receive while singing Schubert's melodious lieder truly lacks parallel. As I flow through each lyric German verse, I can hardly control my shivers, convinced that Schubert wrote his famous song cycles specifically for me.

The unsurpassed beauty of classical music, in all forms, from opera to chamber music, and by every composer, from J. S. Bach to Giacomo Puccini, has the power to explore human emotion at its most natural state, the way no written work could ever hope to do. This music brings love, anger, excitement, and splendor to the earth. And yet, I was embarrassed of my ability to admire it. As time went by and my love for classical music developed and matured, along with my character, I realized the importance of sharing my love of beautiful music with others. Perhaps other people would begin to appreciate it as well. Now, I am completely comfortable telling people about my favorite music genre. Even if it may occasionally spawn a confused look, I can still see Mozart's image before me—and this time, he is smiling.

- 465 words
- 4 paragraphs
- Response to specific query: "Describe an interest or activity that has been particularly meaningful to you."
- Also addresses topics associated with meaningful individuals, academic curiosities, and cocurricular interests
- Reflections on activity revealed knowledge of a particular subject—music—and a sense of self-confidence and insight into interactions with peers
- Perfectly appropriate given that he used this for an application to a conservatory with hopes of pursuing a career in conducting
- Reveals growth, a maturity, and acceptance of specific passions the essayist is no longer embarrassed to admit to others
- Is this the kind of student a conservatory would find of great interest?
- Would you have expanded upon the impact of this experience, and connected it with academic, community service, or career goals?

- Would you expand on the essayist's use of the "Mozart's image" reference, adding a fifth and new closing paragraph, projecting future goals and potential achievements that would make both Mozart and the essayist smile?
- Would you like to know more about how this meaningful activity might impact college life, general academic and course-specific choices, or career ambitions?

Sample Ten

Although my interests are numerous, my true passions are very few. First and foremost, I have a passion for classical music. There is an indescribable sensation I feel when hearing a soprano glide through the "Queen of the Night" aria from Mozart's *Die Zauberflote*, the Everest of coloratura repertoire, hitting every F gloriously and precisely as a 35-piece orchestra buttresses her soaring voice with Mozart's brilliant score. The last movement of Beethoven's "Pastorale" symphony overwhelms me with the simplicity of its majestic melody, repeating itself through crescendos, building toward an exhilarating climax, only to resolve with one final echo of the mode, softly rendered by a solo French horn. However, the feeling of making this music lacks parallel. When I sing Schubert's melodious lieder, I can hardly control my shivers, convinced that Schubert wrote his famous song cycles especially for me. My love of voice has only been developing for two short years, but it has reached a point where it defines me, and its hold on me is unshakable; to neglect it would bee impossible. The School of Music's renowned faculty will help me nurture this passion so that I can take my art to the professional level. As a student at a classical conservatory, I will be able to find my voice and to mature as a musician. Also, being part of a larger university, I will be able to take advantage of two different college settings for an optimal experience.

Unlike music, my other passion, mathematics and the sciences, has been important to me for as along as I can remember. I have always loved to think logically and methodically, whether I was determining how many candies there were in an unopened bag, or calculating the interest due on a late allowance payment. As I grew older and my fascination with numbers and mathematical concepts matured, I began to contemplate more abstract things, like sound, light, and the universe in which they exist. I want to study and learn what I can about these concepts, perhaps to event develop my own framework and mechanisms, through which I can approach my questions logically. At the Mellon College of Science, I will be able to master advance calculus and the physical sciences, and each thing I will learn will not satiate, but perpetuate my inquisitiveness.

While my two greatest passions may seem dissimilar, they do have very much in common. For example, music theory is, in itself, mathematical. Different scales and chords follow specific formulas to produce unique sounds, and the form and structure of many sonatas and concertos are based mainly on mathematical patterns. Furthermore, both music and mathematics are universal. Both appear, fundamentally unchanged, in every culture, on every continent. My love for music and mathematics defines me, and I cannot picture any college experience that does not include cultivating my passion for both music and mathematics, whether I study each individually, or their relationship with each other.

- 492 words
- 3 paragraphs
- Addresses specific queries associated with "why this school" or "this program" as well as themes related to academic curiosity
- School-specific essay; reveals self-awareness as well as focused academic interests; directly relates interests to a

particular program, evincing how the two would complement each other

- Student is writing about his passions; in my opinion, you can't go wrong with this approach
- Great connection between two seemingly opposing interests
- Would you have expanded a bit more on music, mathe-matics, or science-focused academic and career goals, elab-orating upon how interests or passions can be translated into career goals?
- Would you have highlighted particular course titles and academic topics or added references to particular faculty and their specialties?
- Would you have used additional closing sentences or a new closing paragraph to reveal the potential outcomes associ-ated with "cultivating my passion for both music and mathematics"?

Sample Eleven

It snapped. I jumped. I winced. A warm sensation, as the pain hit and coursed through the back of my leg. The cadence of my sprint, seemingly, broken forever in that one instant. I had pulled my first muscle, the all-important hamstring, at the start of what should have been my most important and successful season to date. Unable to run, let alone walk pain-free, for 3½ weeks, I was devastated. Needless to say, this left me with a fair amount of time to evaluate my situation and reassess my future athletic goals.

It was my junior year. It was the junior year of varsity spring track, the year when you are slated to "bust onto the scene as a new and powerful force in state competition," the year when everything starts coming to fruition, and the year where here I was injured, badly. The feelings of pain, despair and helplessness

I felt that day in early April, when I was supposed to be feeling jovial and in high spirits, were new to me. Never before had I been struck with such an adversity. I sobbed in disbelief as I thought, How can this be? What am I to do? My career is over and it hasn't even started yet.

But, things happen for a reason. After my injury I had time to realize that you must walk before you can run (no pun intended), in other words the little things must get done before even looking at the big things. In seasons past, I had so much taken for granted little things like warming up and stretching out correctly and often enough. I never did it very well and I basically hated it. I just wanted to get to the good stuff, like competing and winning medals. So I figured that I could continue doing the same, potentially, infinitely. The rude wake up call in my left leg at the most inopportune of times silently let me know that this could no longer be the case. Strict warm up and stretching sessions quickly became the core of each workout and competition I did, and they continue to be to this day.

While sitting out for, at least, a good half of my season, losing precious training hours and getting more and more out of shape I often thought of where I could have been had I not suffered my injury; remembering my preinjury gold medals and school records and things. But, I also thought, "What if this had happened at Nationals while I was on my way to breaking a national record?" or, "God forbid, what if it happened in my senior season and I was unable to run for the remainder of my scholastic career therefore nearly eliminating my chances at qualifying for the coveted athletic scholarship that I've been dreaming of?" Thank goodness this happened at a relatively insubstantial competition, at the start of the season. Thankfully, this turned out to be a blessing in disguise, for now I am able to compete during the second half of the season with almost no pain. With self-renewed senses of priority and responsibility, I have further disciplined myself to know that warming up and stretching out, as elementary as they may sound, always come first.

"Walk before you run." Is a proverb I apply to many things, including my sports career. It has helped me learn not to overlook the "little things," like homework or doing chores, and still expect to reap the ultimate benefits and most successful results. Fortunately, I now take special care to do ALL things well, especially in track, although it had to take such a catastrophic event to set me on the right track. Now I can see that the "little things" do matter just as much as the "big ones" do. Hopefully, with that in mind I will finally be able to enjoy the success that I know I deserve.

- 657 words
- 5 paragraphs
- Addresses topics related to athletics, interests, adversity, and lessons learned from failure
- Event-focused essay reveals self-awareness, yet does not focus on academic interests or project into the future
- Would you have expanded a bit more on the "doing all things well" and "small steps before big ones" themes?
- Would you have elaborated upon how athletic interests and lessons learned can be translated into academic or career goals?
- Would you have highlighted how particular lessons about preparation and attention to details might apply to academics?
- Would you have used additional closing sentences or a new closing paragraph to reveal the potential outcomes associated with "taking special care to do all things well," specifically, preparing for the total college experience?

Sample Twelve

Two years ago, I discovered my emotional boiling point in the American "melting pot. Friends and teachers in the U.S. would often ask me, "How hard was it to learn the English language and to adapt to the American lifestyle?" Yet, no one ever asked me how hard it was to lose pride in my heritage and even to be uncomfortable with the sound of my own name. Sometimes, I wanted to answer the later question rather then the former, but fearing the confused look I would get, I never bothered.

Arriving in Washington D.C. at the age of nine, I was a little Chinese child who was not ready for America. I had not tried to imagine what my new life would be like, and I certainly did not have a clue about the adversities I was about to encounter. Eight years later, after many experiences and much realization, I have trekked through the turbulence of being a "foreigner" and making cultural, academic, and personal transitions. As I recall the event, which transformed my self-image, I am still staggered by the magnitude of what others might perceive as a simple act, and by personal accomplishment.

Every year, my high school celebrates the multicultural aspect of our student body with its "International Week" festival. Students and faculty devote this particular week to recognizing the different nations and cultures represented by the members of our community. Many people use this opportunity to celebrate their heritage and the uniqueness of their country. As a result, during this week, student life becomes more exciting with guest speakers and performers, an international potluck lunch, and student-organized fashion shows and presentations. Watching the excitement my peers felt about their cultures, I finally felt the urge to identify myself as well. I volunteered to host a presentation about the Chinese New Year: its history, traditions, and superstitions. While details of the holiday were factual, and they probably amused my audience for the moment, because they were well received, the most powerful influence was on the presenter. The emotions and enthusiasm felt while presenting my culture, as well as presenting myself, was an incredible sensation that I had never had before.

During my first few years in this new world, I lost pride and interest in my ethnicity, spending all of my efforts trying to "westernize" and learn how to speak, write and act like my blue-eyed friends. Achieving these goals during my late childhood caused me to lose focus on my native language and my born identity. High school was when my pride in my heritage had its rebirth. I was amazed to see that my high school was so racially and culturally diverse. Witnessing this kind of accepting attitude from both the faculty and students, and experiencing firsthand the receptiveness of others as when I made my presentation, I regained confidence in being different. In the past, I honestly believed that my origin and appearance were disadvantageous. Nowadays, I am very proud to be a person of an Eastern origin, for it makes me extraordinary. My culture and personal history give me certain perspectives that others do not have and a unique sense of self.

The renaissance of my cultural pride has transformed me into a different person who confidently sees himself in the mirror and boldly responds to his name. Talking about celebrating the Chinese New Year brought about in many ways a new life. I changed from a boy who struggled to adapt, to an individual who feels no shame to be unique. Finally, I can appreciate my identity and understand who I am. Positive feelings now boil over, as I personally understand how diversity can truly be the right spice needed for any recipe cooked.

- 624 words
- 5 paragraphs
- Addresses topics associated with family, cultural heritage, diversity, overcoming obstacles, and meaningful events

- Reflections on a particular event revealed a sense of self and culture
- Opening directly relates to closing paragraph, revealing who the essayist has become during this period
- Obvious growth; internal changes
- Accurate description of gradual coming-of-age experience
- Essay reveals lessons learned beyond the traditional classroom
- Leaves the reader with the same hope and pride that the writer felt
- What happens next? What will be his next step to continue his journey of growth?
- Would you have expanded upon the impact of this experience, and connected it with expectations associated with college life?
- Would you have connected the essayist's past to future desires to study particular academic fields or enroll in a specific school that cherishes diversity?

Sample Thirteen

It is unlike any other sensation—the feel of the dazzling sun warming my skin as I turn my young face toward the brilliance of a peacefully beautiful summer afternoon. It is the summer of 1991, and as I spend a carelessly happy day with the curiosity and innocence of six-year-old, I am unaware of anything beyond my family, friends, and summer days just like the one before me. I do not think about life any other way besides living in a small one-bedroom apartment that holds my family of four. Who would ever have guessed that a few weeks later we would be stepping off a plane at the Dulles International Airport into our new American life.

Growing up in the Soviet Union during the Cold War, the thought of America floated in my head not unlike some beautiful, vague dream. I thought of America as many children think of fairytale castles—a beautiful thought, but a dream that was so beyond anything that I had ever known that it was nothing more than a figment of my imagination. I had, however, at the tender age of four, announced that I was moving to America to a roomful of my parents' friends. At the time, everyone roared with laughter at my simple notions of moving to another country. No one could later explain why I was so set on moving to America, nor how a simple four-year-old could have predicted the future more clearly than any other adult could. Maybe it was my subconscious telling me that life could hold more for my family, or maybe it was the simple wish for a new adventure, a new quest. I may never know.

When, two years later, I had finally arrived in America, it suddenly dawned on me that life here would not be similar to a fairy tale. My family and I spent the first several weeks adjusting to our new surroundings. We took a trip to the local grocery store and I was amazed to see so much food in one place. I had never seen anything like it before. There were many children my age in our apartment complex and I remember standing by the window crying as I watched the kids playing, knowing that I could not join in their fun because I could not understand their language. It felt as if an invisible barrier stood in my way, and I desperately prayed for the day that I would become friends with those kids, laughing and playing with them to my heart's content.

I had been very eager for the first day of school to arrive but when that day finally came, I was very scared, desperately wanting to be "normal" like all the other kids. This would be the first time that my parents would not be by my side and I realized no one would be able to understand me at school. I felt utterly alone and misunderstood for the very first time in my life. I stood in that first grade classroom on that cool September morning with all these thoughts running through my head. My parents stood directly behind me and my teacher in front of me. I desperately wanted to turn back to my parents for the comfort that their arms would hold for me; I knew I could not. I stepped toward my teacher, just a small, lonely girl filled with determination to make it in this scary, yet beautiful new world, and I did not once look back.

- 591 words
- 4 paragraphs
- Addresses topics associated with family, meaningful events, life overseas, self-portraits
- Reflections on a particular event revealed a sense of self and culture
- Written in a convincing voice, uses specific examples to strengthen the story
- Engages the reader, enabling us to immerse ourselves in the feelings, fears, and dreams of this little girl
- Reader learns a great deal about this student and how she may add to the diversity of a campus
- Could develop a bit more; how will she carry the lessons she learned when she goes to college?
- Would you have used additional closing sentences, or a fifth and closing paragraph to metaphorically link the essayist's first day of school in the United States to his/her first day of college?
- Would you have connected the essayist's evolution from a scared student to a successful one with her future expectations and desires, perhaps using school-specific references?

Sample Fourteen

When I contemplated writing this essay, I was scared, very scared. For some reason, I am very uncomfortable writing about myself. To explain yourself to someone means that you have to know who you are. Unfortunately, I don't think I know myself that well. Well, I do know my name, so I guess that is the best place to start. I have two last names because my mom kept her maiden name, when she and my father married. Since my parents couldn't decide on one, they gave me both, placing a hyphen between them.

Frankly, having two last names is a hassle. There are more letters for people to confuse and a greater chance to have my name misspelled or mispronounced. My massive moniker makes filling out forms very challenging. There is never enough room for my entire name on the bubble sheets of standardized tests. I have no doubt that my lengthy multicharacter number-2 pencil entries cause computer malfunctions, as my SAT scores elicited a large collection of college letters addressed to an amazing number of incorrectly spelled variations of my name. I kid you not. Honestly, I'm not sure that the letter I received from this school was really addressed to me. Well, I'm applying anyway.

One of the things that I like to do is complain. Could you tell? Obviously, sometimes I get annoyed about the little things in life that you can't control, but I work on not voicing those concerns quite as forcefully as I used to. Recently, I've become fascinated by what bookstore shelves label "self-improvement." Everyone would do well to take time to examine truthfully how they live their lives, what motivates them and how they can reduce stress and conflict. Through self-examination I have realized that I am a romantic. I am fascinated by the emotion that nature and life itself can elicit, and I dream that some day I can find a true soul mate, someone who knows me as well as I know myself, a Catherine to my Heathcliff if you will. I guess that is why I place so much importance on friendships. Friends give you a level of emotional connection that, someday, will reveal your soul mate. Friends will always be there for you and you will always be there for them. But, for me, it's even better to be there for someone else while I look for that special someone.

As a romantic, music, all kinds, is very much a part of who I am. I enjoy both listening to great bands and just playing guitar, although I am a dabbler at best. With music you can celebrate technique and artistry as you convey powerful emotions. When Miles Davis was once asked to explain his music he responded by saying, "If I could explain it, I wouldn't have to play it. Listen to the music it's all there." I guess if I could explain it, you wouldn't have to read any more, it would already be all there, on this page. Is it all there, or did I fail miserably? Fear of failure may be the scariest reason I don't like writing about myself. Well, nobody likes to fail, especially a seventeen-year old romantic with two last names who practices self-examination, but really doesn't know himself well, and who is looking for someone else.

- 558 words
- 4 paragraphs
- Addresses typical "describe yourself" query as whimsical reflections that revealed a sense of self
- Would you have expanded a bit more on music, literature, or other academic or personal interests, then project to the college experience?
- Would you have used additional closing sentences, or a fifth and closing paragraph to expand upon "fear of failure" and "search for another," and "search for self-awareness" themes, reflecting ahead to what will motivate success and self-exploration in college?

Sample Fifteen

When people I meet learn that I have an identical twin, they invariably broach the subject at the first possible opportunity. This choice morsel of personal information naturally slips out, they latch onto it, and then whatever the prior topic of discussion may have been—be it school, music, sports, the weather—it is promptly abandoned in favor of this new one. When I'm actually with my brother, this chain of events can be even more truncated, as a simple glance at us as we approach is enough to set people off with their questions. "Are you two twins?" the person might begin. Or maybe he or she will open with the much-used quip (which is apparently never less than hysterical to the party who proffers it), "Am I seeing double?" Of course, one must chuckle out of propriety and restrain any urge to audibly groan. How could they understand my perspective? In the relatively short span of seventeen years, I already have encountered this situation countless times. Even taking into account the fuzzy memory and recognition that, for the first third of this period, my parents most certainly shouldered this trying task in my place (me being just a tot and all), estimates still would be daunting. All my life I have been an identical twin, and all my life people have been endlessly fascinated by this.

After I have validated their suspicions by affirming my twinhood, the next question is almost always, "What's that like?" or the subtle variant, "Do you like it?" The appropriate reply to this question on my part remains a dilemma. With the first wording ("What's it like?"), the basic generality of it has always provided me with ample mental leg room to make simply describing the "ins-and-outs" of being a twin an option. With the other case, the second wording ("Do you like it?"), however, one arrives at a philosophical impasse. I am faced with an evaluative judgment on my present situation to which I have no real point of comparison. I can blithely spout off several little things I may superficially like or dislike—the wonders of fraternal telepathy, say, or the headaches of sibling rivalry—but can I really speak to whether or not being a twin should be placed in the pro or con column of my life? My existence as a twin is so fundamental, so inherent to my being that I could never truly answer. And so all I can respond with is a tentative "Well . . . fine, I guess. I can't complain, and I'm content."

Though in moments of anger I have often seen fit to call my twin brother useless and annoying, this pronouncement would never hold. His role in my life, no doubt, has been integral. (At the very least, his identical genetic make-up has always offered me the perfect organ repository should I ever need a transplant.) Including a cushy nine months straight in the inviting confines of the womb, there is no other person in the world I have spent more time with than Paul. When we are together, I know of no other person I can be around and yet proceed to act so naturally and so uninhibitedly that it seems as if I were by myself. So, when people eventually get around to asking me "Do you two fight a lot?" or "Do you guys get along with each other?" (customarily their third or fourth question), the answer is simple. While we may have occasional little quarrels, my brother and I are best friends. Our fights, short-lived and insignificant, never surpass inane bickering and squabbling; their cause is usually no deeper than a bout of misplaced frustration or fatigue-induced crankiness, which I'm sure everyone has felt at one time or another.

Perhaps the most sensible explanation for why we get along so remarkably well is supremely self-evident. Simply put, my brother and I understand each other better than anyone else. We laugh at the same jokes and strange observations, and we share the same interests. That we often can anticipate each other's actions and thoughts does not qualify as some supernatural power, but merely speaks to how similar our sensibilities are. To me, this wonderful connection is what has always made my relationship with my twin brother special. Indeed, because of it, I have never been able to fathom how a set of twins could be less than harmonious.

- 739 words
- 4 paragraphs

- Addresses topics associated with family, influential people, and self-portraits
- Reveals a maturity of perspective and approach to interacting with others
- Would you have added a sentence or two addressing how "twinhood" will influence the college experience and impact the essayist's expectations?
- What did you learn about the essayist as you read this piece, and what more do you want to know?
- Can you envision someone writing a similar piece about an older or younger sibling, about a teammate, or about a significant relationship?

As you read these samples, did you seek to learn something special about each essayist? Did you find any grammatical errors, typos, or subtle mistakes? Would you make additions or changes to any? Did you circle errors, highlight particularly good sentences or paragraphs, or make comments or queries in the margins? Did you answer all of the questions posed at the beginning of the chapter for each of the samples? If you did, great! You've definitely developed the eyes, heart, and head of the essayist and of the editor.

Very soon, you will use these qualities to review, revise, and finalize your own drafts. Before you do, we will examine how one essayist revised and improved upon an essay. Step by step, you will learn how an initial draft is critiqued to create revised versions and, finally, the finished product. I know that you're now eager to start writing, inspired by the samples in this chapter, but do progress to the next before you put pen to paper or fingers to keyboard.

Some of you may feel a bit intimidated by what may seem to be "unique" experiences of those who wrote the essays appearing in this book. Don't be. Each of you, as self-assessment will reveal, has unique qualities and experiences worthy of sharing through your essays. You are amazing individuals, with amazing stories to tell. Tell them with passion and structure in your own well-crafted admissions essays.

Special appreciation is offered to those who shared these samples. While some of the submitted essays may not have appeared in this book, every individual cited in this book's dedication is a personification of success and deserving of recognition.

9 A Before-and-After
Review and Comprehensive Critique

WE'VE ALL HEARD THAT a picture is worth a thousand words. But how many illustrations are needed to maximize your use of about 500 to 700 words? You've already reviewed and analyzed quite a few samples, so you've seen the results of much effort. When reading samples, you identified styles as well as content and used strategic questions to assess the quality of each essay. Now, let's gain a glimpse into the process that facilitates the transformation of first drafts into finished essays. The nature of this "before-and-after review" should inspire you to seek the feedback of others while creating your own essays. Remember, you are the one applying for admissions, and only you should truly write your essays. It is appropriate, however, to seek the editorial as well as the motivational support of others.

This student-to-essay coach scenario will clarify as you progress page by page. When you review comments of the coach and responses of the essayist, as well as varied drafts of the essay, reflect upon editing questions first posed in Chapter 5. These critiquing queries you'll see here are among those a coach might ask. If you don't have a support person, use self-inquiries, responses, and subsequent revisions to help you develop the very best essay.

The following bulleted questions can facilitate effective progress from draft to final version. If you have been working on your own up until now, use these questions as a verbal checklist. When you do have someone helping with editing, it will be valuable to ask these questions together as you review and revise drafts. Within these questions are the answers you seek.

Revising: Adding, Improving, and Deleting

When you progress through essay writing ABCs, from Drafting, through Editing, to Finalizing, critiquing guidelines and checklists can be extremely helpful. Editing is a critical step, so use whatever help you can.

- Review the draft paragraph by paragraph.
- Did you follow your plan, with each sentence and paragraph revealing a clear purpose?
- Did you respond to the topic?
- Do the introductory, supporting, and concluding paragraph serve desired purposes, or should they be revised and reordered?
- Does the essay appear in a logical order and, ultimately, project a sense of unity?
- Does the essay reflect values, interests, and personality?
- Does the essay follow the predetermined structure?

Revising: Fine-Tuning

While most writers don't like to admit it, traditional editorial queries do inspire creative copy and yield the best results. Assistance when finalizing your essay can be critical.

- Review this draft sentence by sentence.
- Do the topic sentences in each paragraph serve desired purposes, or should they be revised, reordered, or removed?

- Do the supporting and transition sentences in each paragraph serve desired purposes, or should they be revised, reordered, or removed?
- Do the thesis and concluding sentences serve desired purposes, or should they be revised?
- Does the essay remain in proper tense and voice, focusing clearly on the target reader?
- Does the essay present the most important points among those outlined in prewriting and planning?

Proofreading

The last of the six steps to essay writing success must include detailed proofreading. You don't want all of your hard work to be negatively impacted by simple and easy to correct errors.

- Review this draft word for word.
- Does the essay follow rules of grammar and usage?
- Is it free of typos and spelling errors?
- Does it contain the correct references to school name, place, and institution-specific information?
- Do all of your supporting details show in the final draft?
- Do any revealing techniques maximize the sense of surprise, creativity, or humor?
- Do the vocabulary words express all points and thoughts effectively?

The Essay Coach and Essayist

Essay Coaches can be teachers, counselors, peers, and even, parents. Coaches do not write essays for candidates, but they do inspire essayists to maximize their efforts. They are positive, enthusiastic and, when needed, structured facilitators. Coaches can be involved at every one of the six steps, from Assessment through Finalizing, or they can get involved only in the final ones, Editing and Finalizing. Good coaches exhibit the style and attitudes presented in the student-to-essay coach scenario that follows.

Coach: Of course I'll look over your essay draft. I understand you only have a week to complete this one, because you want to submit it for an early admissions application. So, we'll be direct and focused. Using e-mail will speed up the process, but don't let it lessen your motivations or diminish our back and forth interactions. Feel free to call with questions or if you need clarification. What is the question that you will be answering? When will you get me your first draft?

Essayist: I think I'm going to answer the question about my favorite book. I'll get you a draft very soon.

Coach: Yes, "the favorite book" question is a good one. You're an avid reader. Are you thinking about books you've read for pleasure or for school? Make sure you write abut one that really impressed you, so writing about it will come naturally. Don't force yourself to write about a particular title, just because you think it might be impressive to the admissions people. I look forward to seeing your first draft. Go for it!

Essayist: Here it is. I'm not sure I answered the question the way they wanted. Do I need to prove that I read the book, show that I know what it was all about, or what?

Coach: Got the draft. Will review and send back my initial comments ASAP!

Draft One

The novella *Schachnovelle*, by Stefan Zweig is most definitely the book that has left the greatest impression on me. Before telling you why, though, let me introduce the author and provide you with some background information. Stefan Zweig was born in 1881 in Vienna and lived in Salzburg, England, USA, and Brazil. This book made him world famous, but he wasn't able to prosper from his fame, since he committed suicide in February 1942 in Petropolis, Brazil.

On a passenger boat from New York to Buenos Aires, a millionaire challenges the world champion in chess, Mirko Czentovic, to play a game of chess with him. In return he promised him money. During the game the passenger Dr. B, the key character of the book, helps the millionaire and earns the respect of the world champion, who challenges him right away. In the course of the book the reader finds out about Dr. B's past: During the second world war he had been held prisoner in a hotel room, by the Gestapo. He is totally isolated and his mind hungers for knowledge. One day he is able to steal a book, which to Dr. B's regret, happens to be a book of 150 chess games. The book powerfully describes the paths his mind undergoes in order to be able to visualize the games in his head. Completely taken up by this activity, he becomes sick with a psychological disease and a nervous breakdown and is therefore released from captivity. This is his first chess game after these events and he manages to beat Czentovic, but while playing the second game, the past catches up with him and takes control, he starts talking in a confused manner and is only saved by a friend, the narrator, who he had meet on the ship. He stops playing right away, with the determination to never play again.

It is not very easy to describe why I like the book, one just has to read it and he, too, will be spellbound by the way Stefan Zweig has described the captivity of Dr. B. He becomes totally schizophrenic because he has to imagine two players and there moves, while not being allowed to know what the other one is doing.

It shows the thirst for knowledge of the mind and how a human being is not able to live in total isolation, but it also shows that there is always hope and a future, that is too precious to give up. The Schachnovelle is a story, which I will never forget.

Coach: Good first draft. It's about 425 words and contains four paragraphs. Great start. Before I comment on this draft, and make some specific suggestions, I do have a few questions. Okay? Here goes . . .

- When did you read this book?
- Did you read it in English or German?
- Did you read it for school or pleasure?
- If for school, have you written any essays about the book prior?
- Do you relate to the statement you made about the book in this first draft: "It shows the thirst for knowledge of the mind and how a human being is not able to live in total isolation but it also shows that there is always hope and a future, that is too precious to give up"? Haven't you demonstrated a thirst for knowledge and an aversion to isolation? Can you relate to this character?
- What was it about the author's description of Dr. B's captivity that intrigued you so much?
- Which schools do you now think you will apply to?
- Which schools will you use this essay for?
- Did you write the essay in German, and then translate to English, or just in English?

Before I make my comments, look at the draft you wrote and think about what you would add to revise your essay and what would reveal more about you and your current academic and personal goals. After I get your responses I will be prepared to make some specific suggestions. I look forward to getting your next e-mail soon. Remain focused, but don't get too worked up. We still have five days. That's plenty of time if we keep our communications flowing day to day.

> Essayist: Here are my answers to your questions. I hope they are what you are looking for:

It was one of those books you had to read without putting it down. He described in much detail the changes that Dr. B experienced in order to play chess with himself. There was really very little action in the book. I would say 80% of the book took place solely in Dr. B's room. I almost want to say that the author wrote with the intent to influence the reader's mind in some fashion, trying to in some way create the same confusion and emotion that Dr. B felt. I was uncomfortable while reading the book, but I was driven to finish, because I wanted to find out what happened to the characters and because I wanted to work through the feelings it inspired.

I'm now thinking about a whole range of schools to apply to including Dartmouth, Yale, Princeton, University of Rochester, SUNY Geneseo, SUNY Potsdam, SUNY Albany, SUNY Buffalo, and SUNY Binghampton. This particular question is for Yale, Princeton, and Rochester, but I might adapt it for a few others. Is that appropriate? Don't I have to answer all the questions directly?

I wrote the essay in English and whenever I didn't know a word or phrase, which happened quite a lot, I had to look it up. It's not as easy being bilingual as some people think. I would definitely be more comfortable writing my applications in German, but I realize that's not allowed. I'm doing the best I can. Any ideas?

I guess I should include a little more about myself. Should I stress the fact that this book was read in an English class, while I attended school in Germany? I did not mention anything about my background in the essay, because there are other questions in my applications that cover that area already. Do you think I should tie the points I make in my essay to my personal life? For example, as one of your questions pointed out, I can link Dr. B's personality to my own and also explain to the reader why I found the book so memorable. Describing a specific scene from the book or citing a phrase that was dominating could help to make the essay less generic. Would that be a good idea? What made the book so fascinating was how the author shared with readers the path from one normally functioning brain to two different personalities. It might be cool to explore this a bit more.

Coach: Interesting answers. You did a great job thinking about the questions I posed. Now based on your answers, particularly to the last question, you are ready to write another draft. Before you do, I have some specific suggestions, comments, and a few more questions:

- Don't rephrase the question in the first sentence of your revision. Start with a statement that will pique the curiosity of the reader.
- Yes, do share with the reader that the book was read in an English class, while you lived and attended school in Germany. In logical and descriptive ways share things about your background and how your experiences might relate to those in the book.
- Most definitely parallel Dr. B's personality and yours.
- Don't worry about length for the next draft. Go beyond the 600-word limit if you have to. We can always edit down the final version.

Essayist: I get it! You want more of me in the essay and you want me to project myself into the book. You want the reader to know more about me, not as much about the author and the plot. Right?

Well, I tried to put more of me in this next draft. How did I do? I think it's great and my mom thinks it's great. Is it finished? Can I send it off to the schools? I've got so many other things to do, I want this essay and the application done. Help!

Draft Two

While I have read many books, there are only a few I recall over the years. One of those books was the Schachnovelle, in English, chess novella, by Stefan Zweig. I read this book in 10th grade while living in Kiel, Germany, and the first thing that impressed me about the book, even before having read the book itself, was the author. Stefan Zweig was born in 1881 in Vienna and lived in Salzburg, England, USA, and Brazil. He reminded me of myself to some extend and also how I would like my life to look in the future. I had grown up in Germany and then moved to Port Jefferson, NY, for the duration of Middle School and had then returned to my hometown in Germany. However, my real fascination with the book was due to the interesting story line of the Schachnovelle. On a passenger boat from New York to Buenos Aires, a millionaire challenges the world champion in chess, Mirko Czentovic, to play a game of chess with him. During the game, the passenger Dr. B, the key character of the book, helps the millionaire and earns the respect of the world champion, who challenges him right away. In the course of the book the reader finds out about Dr. B's past.

During the Second World War the Gestapo held him prisoner in a hotel room. In his isolation, his mind began to hunger for knowledge of any sort. One day he was able to steal a book, which to Dr. B's regret, happened to be a book of 150 chess games. The author goes on to powerfully describe the paths Dr. B's mind underwent in order to be able to visualize the chess games in his head. Completely taken up by this activity, he became sick with a psychological disease and a nervous breakdown and was therefore released from captivity. Since then, Dr. B had not played another game of chess, however he is able to beat Czentovic on the ship. During the course of the second game, the past catches up with Dr. B and takes control. He starts talking in a confused manner and is only saved by a friend, the narrator, whom he had met on the ship. He stops playing right away, with the determination to never play again.

The author is able to describe what happens to Dr. B in such a precise manner, that it simply captivates the reader. On a more personal level, I was also able to relate to the main character, because I, too, have a strong thirst for knowledge and believe that it is essential to relate to other people and interact vs. living in isolation. Dr. B doesn't give up hope, even though he finds himself in a more than complicated situation. He resolves his problem by adapting and becoming two players at the same time to complete the game of chess. Even though, he pays a high price for this adaptation, his healthy mind, it was the best solution for his problem of isolation. Last, but not least, it is the very descriptive manner in which Zweig describes the events of the story that make this book unforgettable to me.

Coach: This draft is 537 words, and only three paragraphs. Good job! Much improved. Yes, you've guessed my not-so-subtle approach to coaching you through this process. Your essay must reveal things about you. It must show readers that you can express yourself in your non-native tongue, English, and must reveal things about you that the other sections of the applications cannot. Your essay is more than just a writing sample. While the essay question asked about a "favorite book," you want to reveal as much about you as you do about the book. I don't think admissions professionals really want essays that analyze books. They are not creating a suggested reading list. They want to analyze applicants in order to admit those who will succeed and contribute to their academic communities. No matter what the question, think about what you can share in order to support your candidacy. Make sure you answer the question, but don't limit your responses to information about books, events, or about others. The key is revealing something about yourself while addressing essay questions and topics posed.

This second version is much, much better. I agree with those who have read it and who like it. But, I don't think it is quite done. I have a few additional subtle, and not-so-subtle comments, suggestions, and questions.

- Describing a specific scene from the book or citing a particular phrase would be a good idea.
- Isn't learning English in Germany and now living as a dual German–United States citizen in the U.S. a bit like having two personalities?
- Doesn't the English-German language issue often make you feel as if you are like two people, playing "word chess" against yourself?
- Are there any other parallels between you and the author and you and the characters?

Now think about these questions and comments and write another draft. Remember, save the second one as a separate document in your system, and then create a new document to use for the next draft. Just use the "save as" command and name the next one "draft three." Don't just revise by working over the existing document. Just in case we don't like the third draft as much as the second, or the fourth as much as the third, you want archives of all previous versions. You are very, very close to being done. Stay positive, enthusiastic, and focused. Let's try to finish it by tomorrow, so you can do some very thorough proofreading, have someone else review the final version, finish the essay, make copies of all admissions documentation, and send in the entire packet a few days prior to the deadline.

Essayist: Okay. I understand your newest suggestions and your questions. This next draft should not take too long. I'll get a new version back later in the day. Are we close to being done? I do have a lot of schoolwork to focus on and the deadline for the early admissions application is fast approaching. As you might be able to tell, I'm getting a bit anxious.

Okay. Here's the next version. I think it's exactly what you want. As you will see I added some things to the essay on the bottom to incorporate the questions you had posed.

Draft Three

While I have read many books, there are only a few I recall over the years. One of those books was the Schachnovelle, in English, chess novella, by Stefan Zweig. I read this book in 10th grade while living in Kiel, Germany, and the first thing that impressed me about the book, even before having read the book itself, was the author. Stefan Zweig was born in 1881 in Vienna and lived in Salzburg, England, USA, and Brazil. He reminded me of myself to some extent and also how I would like my life to look in the future. I had grown up in Germany and then moved to Port Jefferson, NY, for the duration of Middle School and had then returned to my hometown in Germany.

However, my real fascination with the book was due to the interesting story line of the Schachnovelle. On a passenger boat from New York to Buenos Aires, a millionaire challenges the world champion in chess, Mirko Czentovic, to play a game of chess with him. During the game, the passenger Dr. B, the key character of the book, helps the millionaire and earns the respect of the world champion, who challenges him right away. In the course of the book the reader finds out about Dr. B's past.

During the Second World War the Gestapo held him prisoner in a hotel room. In his total isolation, his mind began to hunger for knowledge of any sort. One day he was able to steal a book, which to Dr. B's regret, happened to be a book of 150 chess games. The author goes on to powerfully describe the paths Dr. B's mind traveled in order to be able to visualize the chess games in his head. Completely taken up by this activity, he became sick with a psychological disease and a nervous breakdown and was therefore released from captivity. Since then, Dr. B had not played another game of chess, however he is able to beat Czentovic on the ship. During the course of the second game, the past catches up with Dr. B and he takes control. He starts talking in a confused manner and is only saved by a friend, the narrator, whom he had met on the ship. He stops playing right away, with the determination to never play again.

The author is able to describe what happens to Dr. B in such a precise manner, that it simply captivates the reader. On a more personal level, I was also able to relate to the main character, because I, too, have a strong thirst for knowledge and believe that it is essential to relate to other people and interact vs. living in isolation. Dr. B doesn't give up hope, even though he finds himself in a more than complicated situation. He resolves his problem by adapting and becoming two players at the same time to complete the game of chess. Even though, he pays a high price for this adaptation, his healthy mind, it was the best solution for his problem of isolation. Furthermore, Dr. B' duality is very similar to my own duality of being a German citizen living in the US. Sometimes, I, too, feel as if I was two people. Even though the American and the German culture are very similar, there are distinct differences, such as the overall attitude toward life.

Whenever I am asked if I feel more American or German I don't quite know how to answer, since I am both of them at the same time. The fact that Zweig is able to describe so closely and accurately what Dr.B's duality is like amazes me, since I have never been able to describe my own situation in such a fashion. This makes the book an unforgettable one.

Coach: This draft is 633 words, and now four paragraphs. It's great. It's a little bit long, but great. We can edit down the thirty or so words later. I sincerely hope it's what you want, not necessarily what I want. Remember, the essay must reflect you and reveal to readers something the application may not have revealed. Yes, it does show how well you write, but it should also show who you are. Let's save this one, the third draft, exactly as is. It may be the "finished and final copy" that you send to these schools. Really, it's a good essay. Sincerely, it's almost a great essay! I've made some proofreading and editorial markings on the draft I'm sending back. Before you make any changes, save this version in case it proves to be the one you like best. Once you correct it, do save the revised version as well. Both might be "finished essays," but you can make the decision regarding which one to submit later. Let's take a whole new direction with the next draft. It won't take that long. We're close to the end, so don't lose momentum or your great attitude. You are doing great!

Draft Three with Editorial and Proofreading Markings
While I have read many books, there are only a few I recall ~~over the years~~ vividly. One of those books was the Schachnovelle, ~~in English, chess novella,~~ by Stefan Zweig. I read this <u>chess novella,</u> <u>written in English,</u> ~~book~~ in 10th grade while living in Kiel, Germany~~, and.~~ ~~the first thing that impressed me about the book, even~~

~~before having read the book itself, was the author.~~ Stefan Zweig was born in 1881 in Vienna and lived in Salzburg, England, <u>the</u> USA<u>,</u> and Brazil. He reminded me of myself to some ~~extend~~ <u>extent.</u> ~~and also how I would like my life to look in the future.~~ I had grown up in Germany and then moved to Port Jefferson, NY, for the duration of Middle School and had then returned to my hometown in Germany. <u>Zweig's travels and multinational experiences impacted his abilities to understand and communicate with others and accomplish professional goals.</u>

However, my real fascination with the book was due to the ~~interesting~~ story line <u>and character insights</u> ~~of the Schachnovelle~~. On a passenger boat from New York to Buenos Aires, a millionaire challenges the world champion ~~in chess~~, Mirko Czentovic, to play a game of chess with him. During the ~~game~~ <u>match,</u> ~~the~~ <u>a</u> passenger Dr. B, the key character of the book, helps the millionaire and earns the respect of the world champion, who challenges him right away. In the course of the book the reader finds out about Dr. B's past.

During the Second World War the Gestapo held ~~him~~ <u>Dr. B</u> prisoner in a hotel room. In his total isolation, his mind began to hunger for knowledge of any sort. One day he was able to steal a book. ~~which to Dr. B's regret.~~ <u>The book was a description</u> of 150 chess games. The author goes on to powerfully describe the paths Dr. B's mind underwent in order ~~to be able~~ <u>to</u> visualize the chess games in his head. ~~Completely~~ <u>Ultimately, completely</u> taken up by this activity, he ~~became sick with a psychological disease and~~ <u>suffered</u> a nervous breakdown. <u>As a result, he</u> ~~and was therefore~~ was released from captivity. Since then, Dr. B had not played another game of chess, ~~however~~ <u>until</u> he ~~is able to beat~~ <u>won the first game of his match with</u> Czentovic on the ship. During the course of the second game, the past catches up with Dr. B and takes control. He starts talking in a confused manner and is only saved by a friend, the narrator, whom he had met on the ship. <u>Confronting issues of sanity versus success, his past versus his</u>

future, ~~He~~ Dr. B stops playing right away, with the determination to never play again.

~~The author is able to describe what happens to Dr. B in such a precise manner, that it simply captivates the reader. On a more personal level, I was also able to relate to the main character, because I, too, have a strong thirst for knowledge and believe that it is essential to relate to other people and interact vs. living in isolation.~~ Dr. B ~~doesn't give~~ didn't give up hope, even though when imprisoned by the Gestapo, he ~~finds himself in a more than complicated~~ found himself in a life-threatening and, consequently, life altering situation. He resolves his problem by adapting and becoming two players ~~at the same time~~ intellectually and emotionally, in order to complete ~~the~~ cognitive games of chess played during his captivity. Even though~~,~~ he pays a high price for this adaptation, his healthy mind, it was the best solution for his problem of isolation. Ironically, it was what also yielded his release. Eventually, when confronted by the prospect of returning to his dualistic self, to achieve fame and glory, yet mental instability, he chooses to focus on psychological healing and, at last, he accepts the person he has become.

Furthermore, Dr. B's duality is ~~very~~ in some subtle ways similar to my own personality. At present, ~~of being a~~ I am a German citizen living in the US. Other times, I was a US educated student, returning to German schools. Sometimes, I, too, fe~~l~~t and continue to feel ~~el~~ as if I was and am two persons. Even though the American and the German culture are very similar, there are distinct differences, ~~such~~ including ~~as~~ the overall attitude toward life. Whenever I am asked if I feel more American or German I don't quite know how to answer, since I am both ~~of them~~ at the same time. The fact that Zweig is able to describe so closely and accurately what Dr. B's duality is like amazes me, since I have never been able to describe my own situation in such a fashion. This makes the book an unforgettable one, and makes my own

<u>continued search for self-expression, through my secondary and college studies, so important. Someday, I, like Dr. B, will realize who I wish to be and, someday, like Zweig I will succeed as a result of my multinational and multicultural experiences.</u>

Coach: Don't let all the notes scare you. Just react to them one at a time, and make the changes you like. Remember, it's your essay, not mine. I'm just trying to maximize your efforts. Do not make any changes that you don't truly like. Also, change any phrasing to your style and vocabulary. Seriously, I liked the earlier version and you liked the earlier version. Make only the changes you think best.

Once you've made those changes and saved this "revised draft three," let's try to incorporate some of the traditional five-paragraph essay style into the next version.

- Has the introductory paragraph set the scene for the reader? Describe one scene of the book in detail. Or, ask the reader to imagine himself or herself as one of the characters. In a creative way, bring the reader quickly into the book and present chess via a topic sentence or through questions directed at the reader.

- The three supporting paragraphs that follow should answer some of the questions posed in the first paragraph. Information presented to readers should reveal knowledge of the book's plot, its characters, themes, and most important, knowledge of self. Each paragraph should nicely flow to the next.

- The concluding paragraph reveals how the book impacted you and connects this fictional piece to the realities that you now face. If you wish, you can use this last paragraph to present school-specific information or to share your hopes regarding college.

Essayist: First, here is the finished third version with some, not all, of your suggested changes and a few of my own. It's 650 words; a little more than requested. Is that okay? I think I can edit it down a bit more. I still like this one, and I'm not sure whether the next version is any better. It is certainly different. What are the admissions professionals who read these pieces looking for?

Draft Three "Final Version"

While I have read many books, there are only a few I recall vividly. One was the Schachnovelle, by Stefan Zweig. I read this chess novella, written in English, in 10th grade while living in Kiel, Germany. Stefan Zweig was born in 1881 in Vienna and lived in Salzburg, England, the USA, and Brazil. I grew up in Germany and then moved to Port Jefferson, NY, for Middle School and then returned to Germany. Clearly, Zweig's travels and multinational experiences impacted his abilities to understand and communicate with others and accomplish professional goals.

However, my real fascination was due to the story line and character insights. On a passenger boat from New York to Buenos Aires, a millionaire challenges the world champion, Mirko Czentovic, to a game of chess. During the match, a passenger Dr. B, the key character of the book, helps the millionaire and earns the respect of the world champion, who challenges him to a match. In the course of the book the reader finds out about Dr. B's past and witnesses, through the actions on the boat, glimpses into his present and future.

During the Second World War, the Gestapo held Dr. B prisoner in a hotel room. In total isolation, his mind hungered for knowledge of any sort. One day he stole a book. At first, to his delight, and later, to his regret, the book was a description of 150 chess games. The author powerfully describes the paths Dr. B's mind takes in order to visualize and play these chess games in his head. Ultimately, completely taken up by this activity, Dr. B suffered a nervous breakdown and, as a result, he is released from captivity. Since then, Dr. B had not played another game of chess, until he won the first game of his match with Czentovic on the ship. During the course of the second game, the past catches up with this complex yet fragile character. He starts talking in a confused manner and is only saved by a friend, the narrator, whom he had met on the ship. Confronting issues of sanity versus success, past versus future, and trust in another human being, Dr. B stops playing right away, with the determination to never play again.

Dr. B didn't give up hope, even when imprisoned, in a life-threatening and, consequently, life altering situation. He resolves his problem by adapting and becoming two players intellectually and emotionally, in order to complete the cognitive games of chess played during his captivity. Even though, he paid a high price for this adaptation, his healthy mind, it was the best solution for his problem of isolation. Ironically, it was what also yielded his release. Eventually, when confronted by the prospect of returning to his dualistic self, to achieve personal glory, yet mental instability, he chooses to focus on psychological health and interpersonal interactions, accepting the person he has become.

Dr. B's duality is in subtle and less dysfunctional ways similar to my own. At present I am a German living and studying in the US. Other times, I am a US educated student, returning to German schools. Often, I felt and continue to feel as if I have two personalities. Whenever I am asked if I "feel or think" more American or German I don't quite know how to answer, since I am both. The fact that Zweig is able to describe so closely and accurately Dr. B's duality amazes me, since I have never been able to describe my own situation in such a fashion. This makes the book unforgettable, and makes my own continued search for self-expression, through my secondary and, soon, college studies, so important. Someday, I, like Dr. B, will realize who I wish to be and, someday, like Zweig I will share my feelings and thoughts articulately, and, I hope, succeed as a result of my multinational and multicultural experiences.

Essayist continues: Now, here's the other version you asked for. Again, I'm not sure which one is best. The "final" version of Draft Three seems a bit long. It's about 650 words. Can I go over the requested word limit? I do think it's better than the earlier version, but now that I've finally finished the fourth draft, following your newest suggestions, I don't know which one to submit. The fourth draft is shorter, but I don't want to choose one or the other based on length. What do you think? Which one should I use?

Draft Four Final Version

Author note: After some additional and detailed back-and-forth coach-to-essayist interactions, the following version was created. Feedback focused on following the traditional five-paragraph style, while expanding upon the essayist's creativity. In reality, it did take a few drafts to achieve this outcome, and the coach wanted the essayist to have two very distinct options.

Imagine yourself a prisoner, kept in total isolation. Your mind hungers for knowledge, and your heart longs for interactions. One day you steal a book, a description of 150 chess games. To stimulate your intellect and emotions, to escape mentally, you play these games in your head, hour after hour, day after day, month after month, as if you were the two opponents. Ultimately, overcome by this activity and the stress of your circumstances, you suffer a nervous breakdown. As a result, you are released from captivity. Chess at first helps maintain your sanity, but then it contributes to your losing it. This game of strategy freed your body, yet continued to imprison your mind.

Years later, on a cruise from New York to Buenos Aires, a millionaire challenges the world champion to a game of chess. During the match you help the millionaire and earn the respect of the champion, who later challenges you. You have not played chess since those horrible days of imprisonment, and it took so long to free yourself from the shackles of mental illness that followed. What would you do? How would playing again impact you?

While I have read many, there are few books I recall vividly. One was the Schachnovelle, by Stefan Zweig. I read this chess novella, written in English, in 10th grade while living in Kiel, Germany. Stefan Zweig was born in 1881 in Vienna and lived in Salzburg, England, the USA, and Brazil. I grew up in Germany, moved to Port Jefferson, NY, returned to Germany and I am now completing secondary studies in Fairport, NY.

Zweig shares intimate details of one character's past and allows you to witness, through actions on a passenger ship, glimpses into his present and future. This character, Dr. B had not played chess since his imprisonment, mental breakdown and subsequent release by the Gestapo. Confronting fear, yet driven by a chance for recognition, he plays and wins the first game of his match with the world champion. During the second game, the past catches up with this complex and fragile character. On the brink of another breakdown, he is saved by the narrator, whom he met on the ship. Addressing issues of sanity versus success, personal control, and trust in another human being, Dr. B stops immediately, and vows to never play again. Confronted by prospects of returning to mental instability, he chooses psychological health and positive relationships, giving up the past and accepting the person he has become. Chess has now freed his soul.

Today, I am a German living and studying in the US. Other times, I was a US educated student, returning to German schools. Whenever asked if I "feel or think" more American or German I cannot answer. The fact that Zweig is able to describe so accurately Dr. B's duality amazes me and makes this book unforgettable.

Someday, I, like Dr. B, will realize who I wish to be and, like Zweig I will share my feelings and thoughts articulately. Zweig's travels and multinational experiences impacted his abilities to understand and communicate with others and accomplish professional goals. My journey to learning, self-expression and success continues via secondary and, soon, college studies. It's time for my next move. Chess anyone?

You have now been privy to the interactions between a coach and essayist, seeing how one draft evolves to final versions. Which one do you think is best? Which version would you submit to the schools in question? Did you count the words in the last version, to compare size? In case you didn't, draft four final version has 540 words—but length should not be the determining factor. Would your essay contain school-specific references at the end? Would you have played more with the chess references throughout? Or, would you omit the "chess anyone?" closing? Would your essay contain many of the qualities that admissions professionals look for?

While this essayist had some coaching, the candidate submitting the application always makes the ultimate decisions. You too will utilize printed resources like this one and, we hope, individuals serving as coaches, editors, and motivators. Yet, like this candidate, all final determinations will be yours. Upon completion of this book, you should be able to answer, with confidence, all of the questions posed. You now know what to do, and what not to do, when planning, drafting, and finalizing your essays.

Review all tips and techniques within this book prior to and after drafting essays, and seek the reactions and assistance of others. Remember, it will truly be as easy as ABC, as well as D, E, and F! Your own before-and-after Drafting steps to success are just ahead. Editing can be done with others, yet Final decisions will be yours.

Don't ever be tempted to have another write your essays, nor contemplate plagiarizing. Don't be frustrated by comments, reactions, and suggestions of others. Ultimately, it's your essays and your choices. While it may seem as if others are in control, in reality you are in control, and positive attitudes and actions will yield desired outcomes. Hearing the opinions of others can, at first, be confusing. Listening to the feedback of one or more coaches can be helpful, yet initially frustrating. This book has shared diverse views of contributors, your "paperback coaches" throughout.

Appendix I:
Online, Printed, and Other Resources

BROWSING THE SHELVES of various bookstores and conducting online searches revealed numerous titles on the subjects of college admissions and admissions essay writing. In fact, one search yielded more than 900 publications. A review of publication titles, augmented by several discussions with colleagues, friends, and students, resulted in a creative and helpful way to categorize most printed and Web-based resources.

Print resources fit into one of five categories:

Traditional Heavyweights
These are large all-inclusive reference publications that could also be used to develop biceps and triceps. They are usually anywhere from three to five inches thick, weighing about five pounds. They are comprehensive compilations of colleges and universities, offering brief summaries as well as full-page descriptions. Basic "how to" information is often presented first, followed by institutional abstracts in alphabetical or state-by-state order. Many contain special indexes that list schools by majors, size, competitiveness, and other criteria. Popular books in this category include these:

- *College Board Index of Majors and Graduate Degrees,* published by College Board
- *College Board College Handbook,* published annually by College Board
- *Peterson's Undergraduate Guide to Four Year Colleges* and *Undergraduate Guide to Two Year Colleges,* published annually by Peterson's
- *Profiles of American Colleges* (with CD-ROM), published annually by Barron's Educational Series
- *The Complete Book of Colleges,* published annually by Princeton Review
- *The Fiske Guide to Colleges,* by Edward B. Fiske
- *The Insider's Guide to the Colleges,* published annually by the Yale Daily News
- *The Kaplan/Newsweek College Catalog,* published annually by Kaplan

While most of these books are available at large public or school libraries, and some offer Web-based access to abbreviated information appearing in printed works, you are encouraged to purchase at least one of them. Aerobic fitness and muscle toning aside, you then will be able to write in the text or on photocopied pages, note questions in the margins, and create comparison and contrast lists when making decisions regarding which admissions offer to accept. Yes, they also do make great doorstops for your freshman dorm room.

Lists with Special Twists

These books focus on schools for special needs, on rankings, or on so-called "insider information." This information includes anecdotes offered by students, ratings yielded from student surveys, rankings generated by statistical analysis and polls of administrators, and the opinions of admissions professionals offering "what takes place behind closed doors" perspectives. Some are school-specific, presenting information on particular schools; others focus more generally on the admissions process. Top titles include:

- *America's Best Colleges,* published annually by US News & World Report
- *America's Elite Colleges: The Smart Buyer's Guide to the Ivy League and Other Top Schools,* by Dave Berry and David Hawsey
- *Black Excel African American Student's College Guide: Your One-Stop Resource for Choosing the Right College, Getting In, and Paying the Bill,* by Isaac Black
- *Looking Beyond the Ivy League: Finding the College That's Right for You,* by Loren Pope
- *Princeton Review's Best 351 Colleges, 2004,* by Robert Franek
- *The Early Admissions Game: Joining the Elite,* by Christopher Avery
- *The Fiske Guide to Getting into the Right College,* by Edward B. Fiske and Bruce G. Hammond
- *The Gourman Report: A Rating of Undergraduate Programs,* by Jack Gourman
- *The Student Athlete's Guide to College,* by Hilary Abramson
- *30 Frequently Asked Questions on the Colleges: Special Report,* by Frederick E. Rugg

Most admissions and college counselors are sensitive to issues associated with rankings. I join many others in feeling the same way. Way too many moms, dads, and students are concerned about where a school is ranked, while too few are even curious about teaching methods or the philosophies of education associated with particular colleges and universities. While rankings might be good "getting started" points, they are not the only resources to use to create a list of target schools.

Special lists with twists should loosen, not tighten, that knot in your stomach. So, think about how rankings were established, what criteria were used to rate or rank schools, and how special information was compiled. Often, these publications are best perceived as sources of inspiring questions, not as reservoirs of answers.

Exposés and "Do It My Way" Guides

These books offer behind-the-scenes perspectives as well as expert advice on steps required to complete the college admissions process. Some offer general advice, and others focus on how to get into selective schools. A few target specific applicant pools. This category includes these publications:

- *A Is for Admission: The Insider's Guide to Getting Into the Ivy League and other Top Colleges,* by Michele A. Hernandez
- *Acing the College Application: How to Maximize Your Chances for Admission to the College of Your Choice,* by Michele A. Hernandez
- *Admissions Confidential: An Insider's Account of the Elite College Selection Process,* by Rachel Toor
- *Get Into Any College: Secrets of Harvard Students,* by Gen S. Tanabe and Kelly Y. Tanabe
- *Harvard Schmarvard: Getting Beyond the Ivy League to the College That is Best for You,* by Jay Mathews
- *The College Admissions Mystique,* by Bill Mayher
- *The Gatekeepers: Inside the Admissions Process of a Premier College,* by Jacques Steinberg
- *The Truth About Getting In: A Top College Advisor Tells You Everything You Need to Know,* by Katherine Cohen
- *Winning the Heart of the College Admissions Dean: An Expert's Advice for Getting into College,* by Joyce Slayton Mitchell and Ellen Sasaki (illustrator)

Readers must realize that even inside information does not guarantee admissions. It is hoped that revelations of caring authors with interesting backgrounds will, like those who helped create this book, serve to diminish stress and enhance confidence as you complete all aspects of the college admissions process. Publications like these should be sources of inspiration, not causes of consternation. Some tell you about how to get into the "most selective" schools, while others admit that great alternatives to schools appearing on twisted lists do exist.

Admissions Essay Writing How-To's Targeting You

These publications focus on how to write admissions essays. Some contain lengthy discussions on the process and a few essay samples. Others contain numerous samples and little discussion of steps and instruction. Titles in this group include:

- *Accepted! 50 Successful College Admission Essays,* by Gen S. Tanabe and Kelly Y. Tanabe
- *Essays That Will Get You into College,* by Amy Burnham, Dan Kaufman, and Chris Dowhan
- *Essays That Worked: 50 Essays from Successful Applications to the Nation's Top Colleges,* by Boykin Curry and Brian Kasbar
- *50 Successful Harvard Application Essays,* by the staff of the Harvard Crimson
- *How to Write a Winning College Application Essay,* by Michael James Mason
- *On Writing the College Application Essay,* by Harry Bauld
- *100 Successful College Application Essays,* by the staff of the Harvard Independent
- *Real Essays for College and Grad School: Actual Essays to Increase Your Chances for Admission and Scholarships,* by Anne McKinney

- *The Best College Admission Essays,* by Mark Alan Stewart and Cynthia C. Muchnick
- *The College Application Essay,* by Sarah Myers McGinty
- *Writing a Successful College Application Essay: The Key to College Admission,* by George Ehrenhaft

Some books approach essay writing from academic and literary perspectives. They explain in detail various types of essays, as well as the structure, content, and style requirements of technically sound essays. These books regularly suggest the lengthy drafting, editing, and fine-tuning stages of a drawn-out and detailed process. If you think about it, admissions essay writing is not best viewed as academic or as a lengthy process. Admissions essays are your way to share your views with readers and, in many positive ways, express thoughts and attitudes that will yield admissions success.

A few books cleverly make unspoken promises about getting readers into Ivy League schools. These publications project "we've got the secret" attitudes, and reveal the perspectives of a number of college admissions professionals. The jackets of these titles reveal that authors attended Ivies, and that collaborators are associated with selective institutions. So, it doesn't take a Harvard or Princeton grad to realize for whom these books are targeted and the implicit promises being made by text, tone, and style.

Other books contain sample essays, written by those who attended the universities and colleges discussed within the very text of those books. These publications imply that reading essays can, alone, inspire you to write great essays and thus get into competitive and prestigious schools. Most of these books present too many samples. An essay without an analysis doesn't inspire action. But, as you will learn, those with analyses can inspire you to take all of the steps to essay writing success.

You can, and will, write a personal and effective essay! It will be easier and more rewarding than you might think. Reading other essays can be inspirational, but taking the easy-to-follow steps presented in *The Adams College Admissions Essay Handbook* will quickly yield the results you seek.

The Right Stuff to Write Stuff

These are comprehensive books with advice regarding writing and editing, as well as reference publications needed by anyone completing writing assignments of any kind. Most professionals would encourage you to have one of the first three cited and, of course, both of the resources listed in the last bullet point:

- *Get Great Marks for Your Essays,* by John Germov
- *The Elements of Style,* by William Strunk and E. B. White
- *Webster's New World Student Writing Handbook,* by Sharon Sorenson
- Any recently published dictionary or thesaurus

Entering "college admissions" and variations of this phrase into search engines yields tons of hits. Searches using "college admissions essays" as the key phrase yield almost as many Web sites. Web-based resources fit into one of three categories:

Megasites and Portals

Sites that offer general information about colleges, college admissions, and financial aid usually contain links to large lists of colleges and universities, and links to additional information sources, as well as options to purchase books. Novice and technology-savvy users can find large quantities of valuable information and links to many, many informative resources. The most commonly used sites include:

- *www.collegeboard.com*
- *www.collegecenter.com*
- *www.colleges.com*
- *www.college-scholarships.com*
- *www.collegeview.com*
- *www.petersons.com*

Web-Based How-To's for Dollars and Sense

These sites provide support for college admissions efforts and applications with their many resources. Most of these sites provide basic information at no cost, and services for a fee. If you are interested, before you "subscribe" or "sign up" for services, read the costs-for-services information very carefully and ask (via e-mail or toll-free number) any detailed questions you might have. Always check to find out if you can communicate directly with a satisfied customer. Responses to requests for access to satisfied past users should reveal which sites you should find most appealing as well as those you should be wary of. Sites in this category include:

- *www.collegeadmissioninfo.com*
- *www.collegeconfidential.com*
- *www.howtogetin.com*
- *www.review.com*

These sites link users to resources and individuals providing support for those completing college applications and essay writing. While you should be educated regarding all available resources, you must also be warned about some essay support sites. Those following sites, which offer coaching and critiquing services, are your best bet for good advice and tips on how to get answers to your questions or relief for your worries. Sites to be wary of are the ones that advertise essays for sale and encourage you to purchase them. Common sense and ethical standards clearly dictate that you should *never* purchase an essay from any site. Admissions professionals are aware of these sites and they know the nature of the products offered. Morals and ethics, common focal points for essay questions, should forbid you from even considering this alternative.

Sites offering essay critiquing and appropriate services include:

- *www.collegeadmissionsessays.com*
- *www.essayedge.com*
- *www.ivyessays.com*

Also, there are a number of workshops advertised via many of the Web sites listed here and in some of the publications noted. If you are that motivated, or Mom and Dad are that generous and persuasive, look into these options. Remember, no book, person, Web site, or workshop can (or should) guarantee that you will be admitted to a school of your choosing, or that you will create an essay that will ensure admissions. Each individual learns in different ways, and each of you is inspired in different modalities. Use, but don't abuse any of the resources. Be inspired, not intimidated by any of those cited.

Last, remember that English teachers, family members, and admissions professionals can be advocates and assist you at every step on your path to admissions and essay writing success. Don't ever be afraid to ask for help or ask a question.

Appendix 2
You're In! Making the Right Choice

I WOULD LOOK AT HER, and without a word, we knew. Sometimes I would smile, or she would smirk or wink, but we always knew. As Jordan and I visited colleges and universities we quickly became adept at the "is that the silliest question yet game." With no disrespect to those who asked, some queries that we heard over and over and over gave father and daughter a common bond and taught us important lessons. I confess that for entertainment we identified humorous inquiries that seemed silly or, frankly, insignificant. Yet, as an unexpected result, we learned that the right questions do help when determining where to apply and, ultimately, where to attend.

Is there a list of mundane questions passed on psychically parent-to-parent? Sadly, I continue to hear these same queries year after year. Usually, parent questions are so broad and responses so predictable that their value, to say the least, is minimal. The following are responses to many of the unnecessary inquires that too many parents ask during campus visits. The questions associated with these answers are among those that gave Jordan and me broad smiles and allowed us to happily pass many hours traveling school to school.

- Every school has "blue light phones, "escort services," and is "safe" if students use common sense; but all campuses have crime, particularly theft of personal belongings if you leave your door unlocked or your laptop and wallet on a table.
- Every school has clubs, cocurricular activities, and intra-murals offering students alternatives to academics, but almost every student will tell you "there's nothing to do here."
- Every school has an alcohol and drug policy focusing on "education and moderation" rather than "punishment, prohibi-tion, and enforcement," yet no students admit to smoking or drinking in excess.
- Every school offers community service options, and some students actually like volunteering, even when they are forced to do so.
- Every school has a system by which roommates are selected and, if needed, changed; some freshman-year roommates become great friends, while others become the subject of humorous stories.
- Every school has grads admitted to graduate and profes-sional schools and those who obtain jobs as of commencement, but some schools focus on placement and on-campus recruiting, addressing the needs of a few, while others focus on processes and services that truly address the needs of all.
- Every school has residence halls, some specifically for freshmen, some that are newer, some closer to campus, some with nicer bathrooms, and some "cooler" than others (and we don't mean air-conditioned).
- Every school has dining facilities and meal plans, yet stu-dents hate the food and find the plans confusing.
- Every school has athletic facilities and recreational programs available to all students, but many complain that there aren't enough StairMaster machines or that everyone is flirting, not exercising.

Because all schools share common offerings, and each seeks to maximize the comfort and growth of students, no question associated with the previous will truly assist with admissions decisions. While institutions have commonalities, they do have differences. Identification of the differences that matter to you will be crucial. Student-generated questions tend to be personal and creative, as they should be, focusing on individual issues. Very few student queries made our list of often-echoed silliest questions (except for the one regarding whether a particular cable network was accessible on campus). When students asked questions we learned more.

While applicants share commonalities, and admissions profiles focus on similarities, individual qualities must be taken into account when determining where to apply and where to attend. As you will reveal in your essay, you seek specific and individualized things for personal and academic growth because you are unique. As with essay writing, admissions, and, ultimately, enrollment, decision-making begins with assessment and ends with thoughts and expressions inspired by questions.

You should utilize the self-assessment activities in Chapter 3 when examining schools you will apply to and, after you receive offers, choosing the one you will attend. Logically, assessment of personal characteristics, aspirations, and goals should be conducted prior to exploring schools. If campus visits or virtual visits (conducted through e-mail and Web site exploration) take place before self-assessment, it's okay. But, do complete the exercises focused on self as well as institutions before you make any decisions.

When conducting on-campus visits, take time to be alone with students who attend the school. Don't treat your tour as a personal one-on-one conversation, but do maximize opportunities to chat with guides before or after the tour. You can always find some tour guides and students hanging out at the admissions office. Also, after visits, or through referrals of college counselors or of admissions officers, ask current students some questions via e-mail.

Questions you should ask before you complete applications, while you're trying to focus on particular schools, or after you have been admitted include these, which are rarely on typical lists:

- Where else did you apply, and where were you admitted?
- Why did you choose this particular school?
- If you had it to do over again, would you attend this school? If not, which school would you attend?
- If you had not been admitted to this school, what one would you have attended?
- Are there particular requirements you find good or bad, challenging or rewarding, or just plain boring?
- Is there something special I should know about requirements, majors, minors, or other academic issues?
- What have your experiences with faculty and professional advisors as well as peer advisors been like? Which experiences were more productive?
- What was your favorite class freshman year, and what were your two favorite classes overall?
- Of your friends who are unhappy here, what most contributes to their negative attitude?
- Of your friends who are happy here, what most contributes to their positive attitude?
- What has been your most surprising discovery, academically and personally, since you enrolled?
- If I am accepted, why should I attend this school?
- What kind of learner does better here?
- Where do you do your best studying?
- What questions didn't you ask before you applied and before you accepted your offer of admission, but you now wish you had?

You definitely should ask these questions. Before each visit, you and your parents should discuss your concerns about them asking particular questions. Do so politely and remain patient if they express "If I'm paying, I get to ask what I want" attitudes. Also discuss whether it's best to ask specific questions in open group forums, smaller venues, privately, or not at all. Have a plan. While you should find time alone to speak with currently enrolled students, parents might find a few minutes alone with admissions professionals, residential or student life staff, or with faculty members. In fact, if you give parents a sincere "to do" list, they'll be happy and productive.

Avoid elbows in the ribs and angry glares. Previsit discussions should clarify what's "acceptable" or "embarrassing," and who can ask which questions. Distractions caused by disagreements or embarrassment will diminish your abilities to collect the important information needed to ultimately make good decisions. Enjoy your campus visits, ask questions, listen to responses, and learn.

After you have been admitted, narrow down your choices and, whenever possible, visit again. Yes, visit again! Even if you have already been on campus, take another trip. If you have not yet visited, you must do so prior to making a decision! Second visits are a common job search practice, yet too few act upon it during the admissions process. Definitely spend a few additional hours on the campuses of your top-choice schools. When you do, ask the previous questions again.

If you cannot visit after receiving admissions letters, communicate by phone or e-mail with admissions professionals, faculty, and advisors. Often, receptiveness (or lack thereof) to your inquiries tells you something about the institution. If you have already visited, you should have some contact names to utilize. If not, a few minutes on the Web should reveal admissions contacts (including directors), student leaders, administrators, and even faculty who focus on student advising and life. Send some e-mails and see what sort of responses you get.

Ultimately, decisions about where to attend will be made after you ask and answer questions about yourself, as well as those about the school. As with essay writing, self-knowledge is critical. Awareness of key personal characteristics, especially learning style, is essential as you make this important decision.

When choosing which school you will attend, ask yourself:

- Do I need structured activities as foundations for a positive social life?
- Do I create my own fun and organize group activities when opportunities arise?
- Do I like to attend athletic, social, and cultural events, including musical or dramatic productions?
- Do I feel comfortable going to an event alone, confident that I will meet someone there?
- Do I feel fearful and anxious or energized and inspired when visiting large cities?
- Do I feel bored and restless or relaxed and focused when visiting small towns or rural hamlets?
- Do I know someone who has enjoyed studying at this school?
- Do I know someone who does not enjoy this school, and who has transferred?
- Do I have a hidden academic curiosity or passion that a particular school can nurture?
- Do I have an overt curiosity or passion about a major or program offered by a particular school?
- Can I attend a particular school, minimizing personal and family financial or psychological concerns? What pressures might be associated with specific schools, or all

schools? Would I feel guilty attending a particular school because it seems too "expensive" or because Mom or Dad won't "approve"?

- Can I create a hypothetical, yet realistic course schedule for my freshman year? If so, what courses will I take, and why?
- If I cannot create a hypothetical, yet realistic course schedule, then why?
- How many of these courses are required and how many are inspired by my academic or personal curiosity?
- Can I express my goals as a hypothetical list of accomplishments for my freshman year?
- What obstacles or motivators might exist at particular schools? Where would I be most likely to translate this list of dreams into realities?

"Do I" questions focus on important self-assessment issues related to college decision-making. "Can I" questions are the most insightful, yet least often asked. Answer all of these questions, particularly the last two. Create a tentative list of courses you might take during your first year. Develop a list of goals you want to achieve by the time the year is done. If you need assistance doing this, ask your college or admissions counselor. While these may appear challenging, and the course selection exercise might take some time, you will be amazed at how much you learn about yourself and the schools when you answer these questions.

Again, please complete or review the self-assessment and institutional assessment exercises in Chapter 3 before making final decisions. The Me That Others Don't Often See and Institution Inspiration and Image inventories should be reviewed and updated at various stages of the admissions process, particularly prior to final decision-making. These exercises are specifically designed to facilitate essay writing as well as the school selection process.

Also, trust your intuition when making this decision. Over the years I have been involved professionally or personally with many applicants who stated "I knew from the minute I set foot on campus that this was the school for me." Campus visits are critical. While some applicants can quickly articulate first-choice preferences soon after a visit, you shouldn't worry if you do not connect with a school immediately. Examination of self and of schools, and solicitation of views of others, particularly parents, are components of a thorough process that will ultimately yield a good decision. For some, decision-making is easy, intuitive, and immediate. For others, it must involve taking into account intellectual, emotional, and financial issues.

Don't forget that your decision should include financial considerations. When tuition, room and board, and related expenses soar, pressures on students and parents to address financial matters multiply. The corporate term "cost-benefit analysis" comes to mind, yet these circumstances often bring anxiety to the hearts of those involved.

Ultimately, determining factors might be dollars and cents, not common sense, or a sense of self. Just remember that if you do enroll in a school that is not your first choice, you have options. Focus on the school's positive attributes—all of the offerings that appeal to you. Start with a positive attitude. You might find this to be the "right" school after all, or you might transfer for the final years of your undergraduate career to your school of choice. Remember, academic performance at one institution can generate merit-based scholarships to another school. Sometimes attending more than one undergraduate institution can be an amazing experience and contribute to an academic resume that is unique and meaningful.

Prior to final decisions, make sure that financial aid professionals are utilized as advocates, not adversaries. Also allow admissions counselors to advise you regarding why you are a good "fit," rather than sell you on the school. Many admissions professionals cherish their one-on-one counseling relationships, so they will be sincere and thoughtful when discussing the admissions process with you. If there is a school you really want to attend, financial aid and admissions counselors can, and will, help. Of course, when communicating with financial aid professionals, parent involvement would be helpful, if not required. Don't try to "leverage" one financial aid package with another, but honestly share your circumstances, and express what would be needed for you to attend your first-choice institution.

Generating open and honest discussions with caring professionals can make a potentially challenging process much easier. It may be awkward to seek advice, and difficult for many to talk to parents, counselors, and strangers about these issues. However, you do have people in your life who want to offer you support, encouragement, and counsel. After you've listened to them, you might be inspired to seek out the views of others who, like our contributors, want to share their diverse points of view.

Robert Massa:

Some students make their college choice by looking at "the rankings." Others seek opinions of friends, families, and counselors. Too often, for many the choice of a college is hit or miss. You will get into a "good school," but how will you choose to attend "the right school?"

Successful college selection must include both knowledge of self and of schools. Self-knowledge comes from exercises like the ones appearing in this book. But, going beyond those inventories, you must think about your answers to the following queries. Jot down your answers whenever you read the questions, so that you may easily retrieve them at decision-making time.

Knowledge of Self

- How do you learn best?
- Are you an independent learner or do you need direction?

When your history teacher assigns a paper, do you prefer a general topic that lets you explore and go in any direction you want? Or do you prefer specific instructions such as "the Introduction must be at least a page long, where you state your thesis, followed by three pages of developing your argument, three pages of defending your thesis, and a one-page conclusion"?

- Are you inquisitive or accepting?

If a teacher makes a statement in class, or describes a mathematical formula or proof, do you write it down and move on, or do you prefer to think about it and question the teacher if it doesn't make sense to you?

- Do you prefer to work and learn in teams, or would you rather work by yourself, memorizing notes?
- Do you find that working with a lab partner, where you can learn from each other, is more productive than studying and memorizing material?
- Are you an active or passive learner?

Do you learn more by being engaged in the process, where you have to think and are often "put on the spot" by teachers? Or do you prefer that the teacher simply tell you what you must know in order to do well on the exam?

- Do you prefer a structured or an unstructured learning environment?

Do you need the teacher to tell you exactly what to do and when, in order to pace yourself and learn? Or do you learn best when the teacher gives you a broad overview of what the class objectives are and leaves it to you to figure out how to get there, asking for direction only when you need it?

- How do you interact with others?

Do you initiate interactions? Are you mostly in large or small groups when you socialize? Do you feel more comfortable when seeking academic or social interactions? Are you quick to start a conversation, or do you listen for a while before responding or joining in?

- Are you an initiator or a follower?

If you are interested in martial arts, but your school does not have a club, will you start one by getting the support of other students and the school? Or will you be content joining the wrestling club?

- What causes stress in your life, and what sort of activities result in enjoyment and productivity?
- Are you fulfilled when there are not enough hours in the day to do everything you want to do, or does that cause you stress?
- Do you prefer to interact in organized groups with a purpose, or informal groups of a few friends to "hang out"?
- Are you open and tolerant of differences, or do you prefer to be with "people like me?"

- If you are a "heavy metal" fan, are you likely to go to an orchestra concert to experience something new?
- What are your general educational objectives?

You don't have to know what you want to major in, or even what you want to do after college. You should, however, know what you enjoy learning about. Are you more verbal, enjoying more subjective areas such as literature or history, or do you prefer the more quantitative, "concrete" areas of study like mathematics and the sciences?

Answers to questions related to how you learn, how you interact, and your general educational objectives will help you understand yourself. This first step is necessary when narrowing choices and, ultimately, selecting the right school. This fact-gathering is best done when determining where to apply. The more focus early in the process, the better. It might make your ultimate decision a bit more difficult, but the challenge of choosing between two, three, or more great schools is one I hope you will have. Once you're admitted, revisit the previous questions and then blend knowledge of self with information gained about schools to facilitate decision-making.

Knowledge of Schools and How They Match Your Personality and Needs

Colleges have "personalities" like we do. Among the characteristics:

- Small or large
- Public or private
- Residential or commuter
- Rural, suburban, or urban
- Research driven or classroom oriented
- Undergraduate or graduate student focus
- Nurturing or competitive environment

- Hands-on learning, small seminars, or lectures
- Diverse or homogeneous population
- Strong athletics community or emphasis on the varsity student-athlete and intramurals
- Large fraternity/sorority presence or predominantly "independent" campus

To discover a college's personality, you should use multiple sources. Never rely exclusively on one, particularly "shortcut" sources such as rankings, guidebooks, and word of mouth. Sources of information include:

Counselors and Teachers

They can help you develop a list of possible colleges that fit your interests, your "style," and your academic profile.

The World Wide Web

Among other things, the Web is a marketing tool, so be careful. Glean all the information you can from the main levels of a school's site, but to really discover a college's personality, drill down to the academic and social department level. Find out what English faculty do in their classes and what projects the public policy students work on. See how faculty and students research together. Get a sense of how teachers teach and how students learn. And learn about how students run their own organizations by visiting the actual Web sites of those organizations. Look at syllabi and assignments. Identify faculty interests and the type of courses they regularly teach.

E-Mail

After searching the Web, e-mail some faculty and students who are doing things that interest you. Also use e-mail to contact your regional (or academic major area) admissions representative and introduce yourself by asking a personal and creative question like those that appeared earlier in this chapter. Don't ask about things that are clearly explained on Web sites or in printed admissions materials. Instead, ask about the experiences and opinions associated with those who attend or are involved in the school. Find out why faculty enjoy teaching particular classes, and why students enjoy enrolling in them. Be curious about their most recent and significant experiences. Ask for the names and e-mail addresses of other faculty, administrators, advisors, and students who might correspond with you.

The Campus Visit

After you have a reasonably good picture of how the personality and program of a college matches your style and needs, get yourself to the campus. Stay overnight, talk with many different kinds of students about their experiences, speak with faculty about their role at the college, and talk with your admissions counselor. If you go to a program put on by the admissions office, take some time to speak with students and faculty who are *not* a part of the program. This will help you determine whether what you are seeing in the presentation translates to reality on campus.

Be objective in your assessments and when evaluating information gained. Don't include or exclude a college from your list because of a good or bad tour guide, because of what your cousin says, or because your friends "never heard of that school." You must take the college as a whole, looking at all of its resources to find out if it meets your objectives.

The Big Picture

If you did your homework when selecting the schools you applied to, much of your work is already done. You understand yourself—your learning style, your style of interaction with others, and your educational objectives. You chose schools at which you are in the midrange of acceptance based on grades and standardized testing score, so there will be many other students like you academically at each school. All preapplication efforts should make the final decision easy, because you chose your schools based on what is right for you. You applied only to those you would be happy to attend if you are admitted and you can afford.

Dollars and Sense

The time has come to make your final choice. Price, of course, should be one component, but it should not be the driving decision-maker. If you are like most students, you have secretly and favorably rank-ordered these colleges in advance of applying (even though I advise you not to do that). That means there are, within your six to eight college choices, some schools you would like to attend more than others. As you make your decision, please be cognizant of how the college fits your style and educational objectives, rather than how much it costs or how "prestigious" it might be. Colleges that are more prestigious may not be right for you because of size, educational philosophy (or lack thereof), and educational emphasis (graduate vs. undergraduate). If the price is close to your financial plan (say within $5,000 per year), the program, philosophy, and environment should dictate your choice. If price is much more beyond this $5,000 threshold, then you and your family need to have a discussion about the value of each institution and weigh the options. Loans and out-of-pocket expenses may, in the long term, justify a higher expenditure of current income for the right fit—one that will propel you into a successful future.—*RM*

Bridget Klenk says:

The thirty or so days between receipt of offer letters and early May deadlines are marked by diverse feelings, behaviors, challenges, and rewards. Some of you will anxiously beg college counselors for any small tidbit of information that will help you make the right choice between two schools. Some of you may feel so confident about a particular school that sending in the deposit check will be a "no-brainer." Some of you may be faced with a number of wonderful options, all of which seem to be right for so many different reasons. No matter how frustrating or exhilarating, easy or hard, when it all comes down to it, you will make the right choice. But, what does "the right choice" mean? Ideally you have applied only to schools where you would like to enroll. So, when admitted to several, how do you weed out all the others, finding the single school where you will spend the next four years of your life?

For some of you, the process may be simple. When speaking with your family, you may decide that for financial reasons, one school is more feasible. I have worked with many students who have chosen a particular school because it would be the most affordable choice. For others, cost may not be the largest issue. You may find that the school's geographic location, overall reputation, the strength of a particular program, size, or other such issue is the main reason for making the decision. I urge those of you who are attempting to weigh such variables to speak to others, ask for the advice of your family, friends, and college counselors, but also recognize that this decision ultimately is yours. After all, you are the one who will be attending the school you select! You will be the one spending at least four years working toward earning a degree and graduating. Your parents will not be there with you, nor will your high school friends. Therefore, you should listen to your intuition and make the right choice for you. Don't underestimate your "gut feeling." Self-assessment is critical at this point in the process, but so is self-expression. Be honest when sharing your feelings with others, and be honest with yourself.

Think about the factors that initially attracted you to the schools to which you applied. Why did you apply to each of the schools on your list? In the college counseling office at Flint Hill School, we use the following Decision-Making Model as well as Decision-Making Tips with our students in order to help them make the decision that is right for them. Our hope is that by learning basic decision-making skills, and applying them to this particular decision-making process, they will be able to use the same strategy for other important decisions.

Decision-Making Model

The effectiveness of decision-making relies heavily on the information available to you. Information is power. The more information you have, the easier it is to make any decision. Often, an inability to choose one path over another is an indication that you do not have sufficient information. The trick is to figure out which information you are lacking and then gather and analyze that information. The following steps will help give you a structure for processing and identifying the necessary information for this decision and others, like choosing a major or determining whether to study abroad.

Step One: Identify the Decision to Be Made

Before you begin gathering information, it is important that you have a clear understanding of what it is you are trying to decide. Some decisions you might be facing could include these:

- Does the academic program meet your needs?
- Is the social atmosphere compatible with your personality?
- Are there appropriate recreational activities available?
- Is the distance from home one with which you are comfortable?
- Is the college an appropriate option financially?

Step Two: Know Yourself (Self-Assessment)

Before you select the college you will attend, you must first develop a true understanding of yourself—your skills, interests, values, and personality characteristics. Questions you may want to ask yourself are:

- Which learning environment is best for me?
- Which geographical setting suits me best?
- What is important to me?
- What kinds of support do I need to succeed?

Step Three: Gather Information and Data

If you have completed the first two steps, you should now have the information about yourself and the schools that will allow you to evaluate your choices. You will now:

- Examine the information and resources you already have.
- Identify what additional information and resources you will need.
- Seek out and utilize new information.

Step Four: Evaluate Options That Will Solve the Problem

If you have completed your research, you are now ready to evaluate each of the options you have identified:

- Identify the pros and cons of each alternative.
- Identify the values and needs that are satisfied by each.
- Identify the risks involved with each alternative.
- Project the probable future consequences of selecting each.

Step Five: Select One of the Options

Based on the information you have gathered and analyzed, you should now be able to choose one of the options.

Do you have enough information to choose one option over another? If not, you might need to do more research.

Overview: Decision-Making Tips for Selecting the School for You

- When making a decision you are simply choosing which alternative is best. You are not making a choice between right and wrong.
- Choosing the right alternative at the wrong time is not any better than the wrong alternative at the right time, so make the decision while you still have time.
- Do your decision-making on paper. Make notes, including a list of the pros and cons, and keep your ideas visible so you can consider all the relevant information in making this decision.
- Mentally rehearse implementation of your final decision and reflect on the outcomes that may result.
- Be sure to choose based on what is right for you, not who is "right."
- Once the decision has been made, don't look back. Be aware of how it is currently affecting you, and focus on your next move. Never regret a decision. It was the right thing to do at the time. Now focus on what is right at this time.—*BK*

Jordan's point of view as a student:

First, congratulations! You have been accepted into college! Now what? As easy as the decision may be for some, it is stressful for others. But, as anxiety provoking as this decision may seem, you must realize that it is a great one to be making. This choice is a reward for all of the hard work you have done in high school—all of the studying and preparation. Before you begin this decision-making process, toast yourself as well as family, teachers, and counselors who have helped you up to this point.

Do not obsess on making the "right" decision. There really is not a wrong one to make. If you are choosing between two schools and are really stumped on which one is better, chances are they would both be a good fit for you. Once you realize that, you can start thinking about the exciting aspects of making this decision, such as meeting currently enrolled students and experiencing the school's environment. To make a "good" decision, focus on fact-gathering first, and feelings second.

If you know any alumni, pick their brains; if you are in contact with the school's admissions counselors, talk to them. Remember, now that you have sold yourself on the school, it is their turn to sell you on their school! If the school allows an overnight visit, take one. It may be awkward, and you may not be thrilled about spending the night with someone you don't really know, but it is better to find out in the spring whether a school is the right fit for you, rather than finding out in September when you're moving in.

I guess my pop has already told you how much he believes in the postoffer campus visit. Try to take the time to visit your top two or three schools after you have been admitted. While on campus do not be shy; ask questions no matter how silly you think they are. If you are shy about asking in person, or if you just cannot get back to the campuses of your top-choice schools, find someone to e-mail your last-minute questions to. Send out as many e-mails as you can to friends, students, alumni, admissions officials, or friends-of-friends. Don't wait until the last minute to collect information and make your decision. Start planning your return visit or your e-mail inquiries soon after you get your acceptance letters.

Include your mom and dad in decision-making brainstorming and when you are trying to narrow down the list to your two favorite schools. When doing so, try not to be defensive or overly sensitive if they give you the "yes, but" stuff. They're just making sure you've weighed all the issues. Be honest about your fears as well as your hopes, the good as well as the bad. If financial issues arise, be patient, but don't be shy about sharing with your parents how you truly, truly feel about particular schools. You don't want to be unhappy and later have them say "I didn't realize that you really wanted to attend that other school. Why didn't you say something earlier?"

Most important, however, remember that this is ultimately your decision, so do what is best for you. You may be feeling pressure to pick one school over another, but it is you that has to live with this decision for at least four years. There is definitely a school out there for everyone, maybe even a couple of colleges that match well with your personality. If you do your research right, and trust your judgment, you will end up at a wonderful school, and be in for a great four years!—*JN*

Loudly echoing the sentiments of my daughter and collaborators, congratulations! You did it! You've been admitted to and will soon enroll in the school of your choice. You identified and explored institutions, completed careful documentation, created wonderful essays, and worked very hard along the way. You deserve much credit and praise. Well done!

For readers at the early stages of the process, who wanted to finish the entire book prior to taking first steps or who skipped ahead, your successes will come soon. For now, you deserve much praise and positive reinforcement for initial actions, including the selection and use of this handbook.

You have reached the end of this book, but have just begun the challenging and rewarding journey that is college admissions.

No matter where your travels take you—campus to campus, draft to finished copy, step by step—your admissions and essay writing quest will most definitely end in success. Then you will begin anew, on the path to collegiate achievement.

Please keep me informed of your outcomes, and let me know how and why the tips and techniques found in this book were of value to you (*bnadler@aol.com*). Good luck!

Index